The fight for quality education is one of the most important battles of our day, for it directly affects not only our children, but our future as well. Winning this fight will take the combined efforts of parents, educators, administrators, and taxpayers. As Bill Honig says, "America's schools *can* be made to work once more. Consider this book your invitation to join in the battle."

Bill Honig has been California State Superintendent of Public Instruction since 1982. He gave up a career in corporate law to dedicate himself to education and earned a master's degree in that field. Before his election, he had been a teacher in San Francisco's inner-city schools and had served as superintendent of a Marin County school district.

✳ BILL HONIG

Last Chance for Our Children

*How You Can Help
Save Our Schools*

ADDISON-WESLEY PUBLISHING COMPANY, INC.

Reading, Massachusetts • Menlo Park, California
Don Mills, Ontario • Wokingham, England
Amsterdam • Sydney • Singapore • Tokyo
Mexico City • Bogotá • Santiago • San Juan

Library of Congress Cataloging-in-Publication Data

Honig, Bill.
  Last chance for our children.

  Bibliography: p.
  Includes index.
  1. Education—United States—Aims and objectives.
2. Education—United States—Forecasting. 3. Education
and state—United States. I. Title.
LA217.H63 1985   370'.973   85-11079
  ISBN 0-201-12644-3

Cover design by Marshall Henrichs
Text design by Robert G. Lowe
Set in 11 point Bembo by Waldman Graphics, Inc., Pennsauken, NJ

ABCDEFGHIJK-DO-898765
First printing, July 1985

✳

_____

TO MY WIFE, *Nancy—my indispensable partner in fighting the good fight for quality education*

Contents

Acknowledgments   vii

Preface   ix

PART ONE   Education—From the Ground Up

1 The Class of 2001   3

2 The Purpose of School   23

3 The Case for
   Traditional Education   41

4 The Excellence Movement
   and Minority Aspirations   69

5 From *McGuffey's Reader*
   to Johnny B. Goode   91

6 The California Experience   109

PART TWO   The Excellence Agenda and You

7 Leverage Points for Reform   129

8 Rallying the Teachers   149

9 How Parents Can Help   163

10 Other Allies: The Universities,
   the Media, the Feds   181

11 Passing On the Flame   197

Appendix: Jobs and Education   211

Bibliography   217

Index   221

✳

Acknowledgments

BEING SUPERINTENDENT of Public Instruction keeps me running from early morning until late at night. Consequently writing a book while in the thick of things would have been impossible without a great deal of assistance. I wish to give special thanks to two people who helped create this book. First William Boly, a man who is as dedicated to the high ideals of education as he is talented as a writer. He's been a pleasure to work with and his professional assistance translating my ideas into manuscript form brought this book to fruition.

Second, to my wife Nancy, I owe thanks for her support, encouragement, insight, and enthusiasm without which none of this would have happened.

At Addison-Wesley, I thank my editor Robert Lavelle as well as Doe Coover, Lori Marsh, Ann Dilworth, and the entire staff of the General Books Division. I'm grateful for their support and belief in this book.

And finally, to the many educators, parents, and students, whose day to day efforts are turning our schools around, I offer my sincere gratitude.

＊

Preface

B AD NEWS TRAVELS faster than good, so they say,
and lately our public schools have had the reviews to
prove it. You may have heard that, until recently,
scores on standardized college admissions tests were going down
faster than the *Andrea Doria*. Teachers have been described as
underpaid, demoralized, or incompetent—or all three. Reading
levels of young Americans fell so low in the seventies that the
Army was forced to rewrite its operating manuals in comic
book fashion. In short, concluded the President's Commission
on Excellence in Education, if an unfriendly power had at-
tempted to impose on us the mediocre educational performance
that exists today, "we might well have viewed it as an act of
war."

So much for yesterday's notices. I'm more optimistic than
that—and only partly because I believe the U.S. public school
system is one of the truly noble experiments in human history
and far too important to the maintenance of our democracy to
be allowed to fail. My optimism grows out of an insider's view
of the most recent national trends. I see a grass-roots, citizen-
backed reform movement taking charge of our educational sys-

---

tem. The people are reclaiming their public schools as places where every student is challenged to grow in character and to perform to the best of his or her ability. The modern prescription for change is a return to the time-tested values of a traditional education: more homework; solid academic courses in literature, history, the sciences, and mathematics; classroom discipline; and, vitally important because it is so often missing, high expectations about what each student can achieve.

I would hasten to add, however, that my rosy outlook is strictly provisional. School reform will continue to happen only as long as a critical mass of concerned people insists that it does. Some forty million children attend kindergarten through high school in 80,000 public schools in this country every day. Such a massive institution won't be transformed at the drop of a slogan or the wave of a magic wand. Rededicating our schools to humane excellence will require hard work and time on the part of tens of thousands of people of goodwill for the rest of this decade and well into the next. But I know of no more exciting, or vital, task facing our nation. In an increasingly competitive and fractious world, how well our children are being educated by our public schools right now will determine the standing of the United States as a technological leader, economic power, and model of democracy through the middle of the twenty-first century. We are talking, literally, about our nation's future. The battle has been joined—our schools *can* be made to work once more—but the outcome still hangs in the balance. Consider this book your invitation to join the fight.

PART ONE

Education—
From the Ground Up

CHAPTER ONE

The Class of 2001

L ET'S BEGIN at the moment of maximum popular shock. In 1983, our school system weathered a barrage of criticism unlike anything the nation had seen since the Russians launched *Sputnik*. In that year, one blue-ribbon panel after another—the President's Commission, the Twentieth Century Fund, the Carnegie Foundation, the National Science Foundation, the Education Commission of the States— weighed in with the same gloomy assessment: U.S. schools were failing miserably at the task of educating our youth. *Time* and *Newsweek* ran cover stories. The television networks aired special reports. President Reagan made schools the topic of his weekly Saturday morning radio program. Then, as abruptly as it had surfaced, the education issue receded from the front pages. The public was left with the clear impression that our schools were in deep trouble. What wasn't nearly so obvious was what we as a society intended to do about it.

The answer is: quite a lot. If the failings of the public schools had come as a huge surprise to those of us in the field, the public would have had ample reason to despair. In point of fact, however, a small band of education activists had about a decade's head start working within the system to change it, and important initiatives were already under way. Three years before the swarm of reports in 1983 riveted the nation's attention, for example, I had begun stumping California in pursuit of the state's top schools job, the office of Superintendent of Public Instruction. The relevant point is that I ran on a platform of traditional education that anticipated most of the national panel's eventual recommendations. And I won, defeating the three-term incumbent by the largest margin in the state's electoral history for that office. By the time the President's Commission came out with its proposals in May of 1983, we had already passed a bill through both houses of the California legislature enacting most of them. The bill was in conference committee, and all we were waiting for was the governor's assent.

If that sounds boastful, let me explain why California's leading the way in education reform was inevitable. According to media legend, California is the nation's trend-setting state. Whether it be hula-hoops or microchips, so the bromide goes, the wave hits California first. Unfortunately, when it came to the decline of standards in the public schools, this old saw proved only too accurate. The Scholastic Aptitude Test verbal scores of college-bound seniors dropped by an average of 19 points nationwide in the seventies, but in California they plummeted by 27. Graduation requirements were weakened around the country in that same period, but in California the legislature reduced them to a single (symptomatically nonacademic) demand—two years of physical education. A typical California student's school life, from kindergarten through high school graduation, was 72,000 minutes shorter than his or her national counterpart's—the equivalent of more than a year of instruction skipped. Whatever category one looked at—the amount of

✳

homework assigned, the reliance on vacuous textbooks, the booming enrollment in such dubious courses as Marriage Simulation, Gourmet Cuisine, or Baja Whalewatch—the California system had become a virtual caricature of the nation's schools in its lack of purpose, discipline, and standards.

What's more, the public knew it. Following World War II, the schools consistently ranked among the state's most admired institutions. But when the Field Poll asked Californians in 1981 to rank thirty-four organizations, the public schools came in a depressing thirty-second. Only oil companies and the welfare bureaucracy inspired less confidence.

With dissatisfaction so widespread, no wonder California was among the first places to go looking for a solution. What surprised me as a candidate was the eagerness with which the public received the reform message once they heard it. I started the race with little more than the idealist's conviction that if your cause is right, somehow you will find a way to prevail. For a year I pounded on doors, talked to just about every newspaper editorial board in the state, and addressed groups of parents and educators. But with little organized support and even less name recognition, I was given no chance of success by the political pundits, and for a while it looked as if they were right. Three weeks before the primary election, the Field Poll showed me running close to last in a group of six candidates, with 2 percent of the vote.

A lot of bad advice from various experts on how to "package" my campaign got me to that point. Fortunately, a whiz kid by the name of Clint Reilly agreed to take over as campaign manager. The first time we met, we had a good talk about the issues. When I stood up to leave, he said, "The people will support you. All we have to do is make sure they hear your message." My wife Nancy and I mortgaged our San Francisco home to the hilt to help finance one last push. Then the spots Reilly produced aired on television, sounding the traditional education theme. The next day, our campaign office telephones began ringing off the hook. I ended up with 25 percent of the primary vote, forcing a runoff, and the rest is history.

Part of me would like to attribute this Silky Sullivan–style finish to charismatic leadership qualities. However, the press was on the job, keeping things in perspective. One magazine profile, for instance, described me as coming across in my TV spots like "an escapee from one of those Brother Anthony Xerox commercials—intense, bespectacled, with a missionary gleam in his eye." It's true, I'm an enthusiast about what I consider the most important challenge confronting this nation. But the larger point is that the campaign prevailed on the strength of an idea. More than anything else, it demonstrated the tremendous popular clout of the traditional education theme. Therein lies the real basis for hope. A vast reservoir of support for the schools is available to be tapped, given a commonsense approach to reform. The traditional education platform is not reactionary or intolerant; it is not radical or apocalyptic. It is essentially moderate, advocating a return to what we know works in education. The fact that the people instinctively back it suggests something to me: it isn't time to scuttle the public schools, as critics on both the extreme political right and left wing are now suggesting. But it *is* past time to correct our course.

By the way, let me make clear that by changing course, I do not mean going backward. The new wave of school reform is not a reprise of the early seventies' "back to basics" movement. As that phrase came to be interpreted by educators, "back to

※

basics" meant a classroom emphasis on drill, rote learning, and the mastery of fundamentals through repetition. Traditional education, as I understand it, implies a much more expansive, ennobling, and—in the best sense—ambitious program.

Traditional education is expansive because it takes as its point of departure the belief that there is a core of knowledge in the arts and sciences that every member of our society is entitled to encounter. Indeed, to be ignorant of this birthright is to be seriously handicapped in the pursuit of the good life—economic, social, and spiritual—which our civilization offers.

A traditional education is ennobling because it trains the mind to think independently—to probe, to sift, to weigh, and to conclude, always with the truth as the lodestar drawing it on. Whereas a totalitarian society indoctrinates, a free society expects its citizens to form their own judgments, as the ultimate expression of their freedom. It is no accident that the Latin word *liber* (meaning "free") is the root of the word *liberal*—originally, a liberal education was one considered worthy of a free man.

Finally, a traditional education is ambitious because it proposes nothing less than the cultivation of an inquiring mind. Mortimer Adler has written that a characteristic of the educated person is that learning continues unabated after formal schooling has ceased. A traditional education aims to awaken the imaginations of students to a myriad of unsuspected possibilities, indeed, to the full potential of their humanity.

It should be apparent by now that this traditional education I support can assume many guises. In practice, however, two hallmarks distinguish it from today's public school norm. First, there is its overall emphasis on the development of a command of language—what the Roman philosopher Quintilian called "eloquence"—the ability to convey to an audience precisely what one has in mind. And second, there is its explicitly moral tenor. A traditional education isn't content to impart skills and knowledge for their own sake. It also seeks to form a student's character according to that pattern of individual responsibility and civic virtue which is the great ethical bequest of Western Civilization.

I am often asked how long it will take to rededicate our schools to excellence. Here again, I believe there's plenty of room for optimism. In answering the question, we can take some small comfort from history: after all, it didn't take long for school performance to fall apart.

Consider those notorious Scholastic Aptitude Test results. The SAT is designed so that, in theory at least, a given numerical score is equally difficult to earn (and therefore means the same thing) each time the test is administered. This measuring-stick quality has helped make SAT scores something of a media darling. Annual results are bannered on the front page as a kind of universal barometer of how well the schools are doing. That's fine, but a word of caution is also in order. Since students take this test at the end of their high school careers, the SAT really gives us a look in the rearview mirror—at how our schools *were* doing over the preceding thirteen years.

With that in mind, let's look at the recent trend. The all-time high average score on the SAT, a combined math and verbal score of 980 out of a maximun 1600, was achieved by the class of 1963. Every year following this peak, the SAT score dropped until it bottomed out at 890 with the class of 1981. For the last three years, the SAT average has crept up a point or two, hopefully signaling the beginning of the long climb back to respectability.

*

In assessing this data, it is worth noting that the period between the acme of SAT scores and the nadir was only eighteen years, roughly one and a half generations of students from kindergarten to twelfth grade. This dramatic slide in academic performance didn't just happen; something caused it. Like a detective at the scene of a crime, we have every reason to investigate what that something might have been, in order to prevent it from happening again. Now that scores are turning back up, the question to ask isn't a disheartened "What's wrong with today's schools?" but rather "What *was* wrong?" Specifically, what was it about the schools in the seventies that turned the youngsters who entered kindergarten in 1968 into the worst academic performers in a generation?

Former Secretary of Labor Willard Wirtz headed a commission that looked into the downslide of SAT scores and issued its report in 1977. One of the Wirtz Commission's findings was actually almost encouraging. It seems that the average had been dropping because more minority students (who traditionally score lower on the SAT) aspired to go to college and therefore were taking the exam in greater numbers. But this demographic trend only explained the slippage through 1970. After that, the most dramatic decline showed up among the best students. For instance, the number of clearly superior students (those scoring over 700 out of a perfect 800 on the verbal part of the test) declined by half between 1967 and 1974. The Wirtz Commission blamed "pervasive change" for this collapse: too much time spent watching television, the breakup of the family, the growing popularity of the drug culture, and the disrepute into which authority had fallen after the twin disasters of Vietnam and Watergate.

Many forces were loose in the post-Vietnam era, no doubt,

but the important thing for our purpose is to determine the concrete form this "pervasive change" took inside the schools, because that's what we can do something about. Diana Ravitch, in her valuable work *The Troubled Crusade: American Education 1945–80,* provides the answer. At the college level, in the wake of student demonstrations against the war, against investment in apartheid, in favor of coed dorms and a variety of ethnic study programs, the most significant change in education involved none of these. "The most important change," according to Ravitch, "was the virtual or complete abolition of fixed requirements, whether of breadth or depth, including class attendance and the time, mode and kind of credits needed to secure a baccalaureate degree."

This loosening of standards at the university level worked its way back through the scholastic pipeline. If colleges no longer required command of a foreign language or two years of a lab science as a condition of entrance, why should high school students sign up for these difficult subjects? Sure enough, a massive shift occurred. Whereas only one in ten high school students was enrolled in the academically lax "general track" program in the late sixties, almost half the student body had taken this scholastic low road by the end of the seventies. Supposedly "relevant" courses like Consumer Math, Detective Fiction and How to Behave on a Date replaced mind-training solid fare like algebra, English literature, and physics. We stopped challenging our children to do their best, and, sure enough, many of them slacked off.

At a fundamental level, the decline of the schools in the seventies was simply the projection of a very powerful—and very wrong—pedagogic theory. The word *education* is from the Latin and means "to lead forth." The traditional education model presumes that, figuratively speaking, one party (the teacher) knows the path out of the wilderness of ignorance and confused passions into which we are all born and that the other party (the student) is willing to follow. But during the sixties the intellectual climate stood this relationship on its head. "School," wrote John Holt in his mid-sixties classic *How Children Fail,* "is a kind of jail and children are subject peoples." In *Culture against Man,* Jules Henry argued that "the function of education is to prevent the truly creative intellect from getting out of bounds." Paul Goodman's *Compulsory Mis-Education,* George Leonard's *Education and Ecstasy,* Charles Silberman's *Crisis in the Classroom*—book after book pounded away on this theme. School was the agent by which conformist society regimented its youth into manageable passivity, stifling their individualism and *joie de vivre.*

The solution was something called "open education," a somewhat vague concept defined largely by what it did away with: tests, report cards, a structured curriculum, and the division of the day into periods and the students into grades according to age. In this enlightened new world, students were billed as the agents of their own learning process; teachers no longer stood at the head of the class but circulated through the building, making themselves available as helpers of the child's experience. (Even in its heydey, open education manifested itself in a full-blown form fairly rarely, but the ideology behind it was both pervasive and influential.) The idea was that if we just got out of their way, the innate curiosity of children would ensure intellectual growth. Indeed, without our corrupting values imposed on them, a new generation of students would blossom into truly superior human beings.

The problem with this romantic vision is that it didn't correspond to reality. As any loving parent knows, children are human; indeed, they show their humanity in a much less inhibited way than adults, which makes them wonderful and refreshing to be around but also leaves them vulnerable to impulsive or self-destructive behavior. One obvious difficulty with putting immature persons in charge of their own education is that they are in no position to judge the relative value of what they are choosing—for example, whether to study astrology (which sounds glamorous and is fun at parties) or biology (which merely explains how the living world works). The difficulty is compounded because sometimes the medicine tastes bad. It isn't easy, or fun, to master the spelling of our language. English orthography is notoriously quirky. Nevertheless, its mastery is a precondition to written communication.

I must confess, I didn't always take such a dim view of progressive education and its radical nostrums. As a matter of fact, I started out as a bit of a romantic myself. There are many good and rational reasons to embrace traditional education, none of which would have convinced me when I started out. In an odd way, my learning curve from progressive to traditionalist has paralleled that of the schools over the last twenty years. We will take on the philosophical merits later, but in the rest of this chapter I'd like to describe what prompted my own conversion.

To begin at the beginning, education is actually my second career. I graduated from the University of California at Berkeley's Boalt Hall School of Law in 1963 with sufficient distinction to be named as a clerk to the California Supreme Court. A few years later, I went into corporate practice with a major San Francisco law firm, but the satisfaction wasn't there. President Kennedy had sounded the call for patriotic commitment,

✻

and here I was figuring out how my clients could save some money on their taxes. As luck would have it, the legal profession had a Constitutional Rights Foundation program underway in San Francisco at that time. Some of the young attorneys visited junior high and high school classes to talk about questions of law: drunk driving, the voting rights act, the free speech movement. When I got into the classroom, something clicked. It was like falling in love. I decided I was going to shift professions and become a teacher.

Part of the motivation was, frankly, idealism—a not uncommon trait of the times. Race riots had torn apart the major cities of the country, and like any thinking person, I was looking for a way to ease racial tensions. It seemed to me that if we were ever going to see real social equality in the United States, it would have to come through education, for a reason as old as Sir Francis Bacon's famous epigram: "Knowledge is power." So I was among the many thousands of foot soldiers who joined the war on poverty; however, I was thoroughly expecting to enjoy it, because I liked teaching.

I joined the Teacher Corps, Cycle 5, a program with the proper ethnic credentials: ten Anglos, ten Asians, ten blacks and ten Hispanics had signed up. We were going to save the world. We read John Holt, we read Charles Silberman, and we believed. We learned how to make individual task cards and personalized lesson plans for each child, and we accepted the importance of allowing the child's natural curiosity and energy to drive the class.

My first assignment was at John Swett Elementary School, a dingy, brick-and-mortar affair located under the freeway on-ramp in the Western Addition of San Francisco. Busing had not yet desegregated the city's schools, and this one's students were nearly all black. The building itself was overcrowded, the atmosphere rowdy, and the climate for learning suspect. The individual under whom I would student teach was the epitome of everything we had been instructed to disdain. Patricia Brigham was tough; she had the commanding presence of a drill sergeant, and you could hear a pin drop in her classroom. She also got results. Her students were reading on grade level—an island of accomplishment in a sea of underachievement. She made teaching look so easy that I had little fear the first day I took over with my progressive lesson plan dividing the class into task forces, each with their own project. To make a long story short, the class blew up. With the least relaxation of control, the place turned to bedlam.

I didn't believe it, of course. Things would be different when I had my own class from the beginning of a school year, I told myself. Eventually, the San Francisco school district went me one better: they set up a group of progressive young Turks (among whose ranks I proudly numbered myself) with a new alternative school. Second Community School, as it was called, did start off with some notable handicaps. Its classrooms were some empty prefab buildings (subsequently razed) in the heart of the public housing projects of Hunter's Point. The people of the neighborhood had been promised the land for a community center and were hostile. One morning we arrived to find that the playground equipment we had put up had been doused with kerosene over the weekend and set on fire. Parents were regularly shaken down between their cars and the school. The police avoided the area, even when we called for help.

Nevertheless, the plan moved ahead. We had 120 kids, half blacks from the neighborhood and half bused-in whites, mainly the children of freethinkers who shared our enthusiasm for open

✳

education. The children called the teachers by their first names. I had responsibility for a class of fourth, fifth, and sixth graders and by the end of the first year was ready to admit something to myself: my students hadn't learned very much. It wasn't for lack of effort. I had spent virtually every waking hour with Magic Markers blazing, dreaming up real-world problems in math, bringing in guest speakers, and watching where each child's interest took him or her and following up with relevant lessons. Unfortunately, a child's interest not infrequently drew him to goofing off; since children are sociable, this tendency had a built-in exponential growth to it. What's more, in the general Brownian motion of the open classroom, the slide toward chaos was nearly impossible to detect this side of a street riot.

That year forced me to reconsider what I had been doing. I was a product of San Francisco's public school system, just as my father had been, and my grandfather before him. When I went through Lowell High School in the fifties, I had studied a structured curriculum of science, history, Latin, English, and mathematics. By then, the place was already a century old and its graduates included people like Dr. Albert Michelson, the first U.S. scientist to win a Nobel Prize: actress Carol Channing; electronics genius William Hewlett; and Alexander Calder, the brilliant artist and creator of fanciful mobiles. Most of the children of the great merchant families of San Francisco—the Fleishackers and the Zellerbachs—had attended Lowell alongside the sons and daughters of bricklayers and cooks. None of these people had turned out all that bad, I thought to myself. A traditional education worked for us; why shouldn't we give at least as good a shot at the common culture to today's children?

That summer, the faculty of Second Community went back to the drawing board. We rewrote the curriculum along more structured, traditional lines. We secured an old-fashioned patriotic history book, *The Story of our Country*. We had math classes sequenced in logical steps so students could progress at their own speed; we taught science, writing, and physical education. Each week a teacher would pick a fine arts specialty and teach a lesson. My wife Nancy (whose new business streamlining the accounting work in doctors' offices was paying the bills my teacher's salary couldn't touch) and I spent Sundays cruising the back streets of Oakland in search of church sales where we would pick up cartons of books for a nickel apiece. Eventually, we built up a library of over 2000 volumes. The kids were taking home books, and we heard about it from the parents. "This child's reading all the time," they would say. "Is he all right?"

Once we had established a routine, we were free to improvise when the opportunity arose. I remember one morning a little boy was sobbing because a friend had thrown his ball on top of the roof. We turned a minor delinquency into a civics lesson. Instead of class that day, we held court. Two students served as the attorneys for the prosecution and defense; another was the judge; those who had seen what happened were witnesses; the rest of the class sat on the jury. A traditional education doesn't mean unimaginative teaching; what it *does* mean is an orderly framework within which innovation can thrive.

The results of the new approach were very interesting. In standardized tests administered citywide, our students scored among the highest in the reading and math tests. But what I as a teacher especially noticed was that they were much happier

✳

as productive students than they had been when allowed to loaf. They enjoyed the challenge.

Governor Jerry Brown invited me to sit on the California Board of Education in 1975, making me the first teacher to hold such a spot while still active in the classroom. Later, I became involved in writing a manual on how to develop a reading curriculum, which became one of the best-selling guides on the topic in the country. Eventually, I returned to the school setting in 1979 as superintendent of a kindergarten-through-eighth-grade school district in Marin County where I absorbed my next lesson in the effectiveness of the traditional approach.

The Reed Union elementary school District had been a lighthouse for education innovation in the early seventies. Whether that meant team-teaching in open classrooms or applying the latest wrinkle in values clarification, Reed Union was sure to be among the first to audition any new school idea. In fact, the district had become quite accustomed to showing curious educators from around the country through its avant-garde operation.

Reed Union had more than its share of superstar teachers, and its buildings were indeed beautiful. The only trouble was that not enough was going on inside them. In its broadmindedness, the district had dispensed with a written curriculum, leaving the small matter of what to teach up to the teachers. One parent complained to the school board that his seventh-grade daughter had already studied Egyptian history three times but had yet to be offered a single course in U.S. history. In the first science class I observed, the teacher suffered a steady stream of back talk and casual disrespect from his students. In response, he meekly plodded ahead with his lesson, apparently unaware that you tell kids as much by what you choose to ignore as by what you say. Not surprisingly, the private elementary school in the area had a thousand names on its waiting list.

I was brought into this situation by a reform-minded board in 1978. The chairman of this group had run for office after he attended a parents' night and heard his daughter's English teacher proudly announce that the children would perform what they had been practicing in class for the last three weeks—the hula dance. My role, as he jokingly described it to me, was to "make sure the trains ran on time." Of course, the trick in managing the educational setting is to establish an authority that is not authoritarian. This means instilling a sense of common purpose, which at Reed Union turned out to be dedication to the ideal of excellence. We put in a sequential curriculum in all disciplines, introduced a centralized science lab in the elementary schools, organized our literature courses around a core reading list of the English-language classics, and bought tougher, more interesting textbooks. (It turned out that we had to buy a junior high school history book for our fifth graders—that's how diluted the content of textbooks has become.)

The indices of academic performance turned up in dramatic fashion. Scores for reading comprehension and mathematical problem-solving skills zoomed upward. A team of our sixth graders came in third in a statewide mathematical skills competition. The hemorrhage of parents withdrawing their children from the public schools was staunched and then reversed. But the most meaningful change was atmospheric. You could walk into a class at random and *know* you were going to find children buzzing with purpose, interest, the excitement of learning.

Certainly, there's more than the Golden Gate Bridge separating the mean streets of Hunter's Point from Marin County's suburban idyll. When one of my best students missed school for a week at Second Community, I tracked her down at home to find out what was wrong. She greeted me at the door of the family flat in tears. Her mother had been jailed on a prostitution rap, and, although only a child herself, she had been forced to stay home and take care of her five younger brothers and sisters. At Reed, if a student missed a week, it meant he was on vacation with his family in Maui. For all the differences, however, my experiences in both places taught me that children, rich or poor, have more in common than not. The truth is, when you penetrate their cool shell of indifference, kids like to be pushed. They like to do their best. We don't have any problem with that concept when it comes to a spit-and-polish school band or a dominant prep football team. Somehow, though, we forget it holds equally true in academics. In that arena, we make the mistake of trying to spoon-feed the material; we lower our sights. I have found that when you demand the best, at first your students will wrestle with you; they'll squirm and angle and look for any leverage point they can use to escape, until they realize you're determined that they are going to learn. Then they'll do it, and do it joyfully, because they know you care enough to make things tough on them now for their own good later.

I'll never forget the time I took a group of "emotionally handicapped" students on a camping trip in the California Sierras. According to the book, such children have basically no self-control or tolerance for pain; they can be very disruptive in class, but I had found that simply getting them out of the city helped settle them down and carried over in a good way into school time. The only food we had for that weekend was what we carried on our backs. True to their reputations, the kids ate most of their rations within the first couple of hours on the trail. As a result, we got hungry come sundown, but not having much choice in the matter, we stuck it out. That night, under the starry Sierra sky, the talk went every which way as we sat around the campfire: what it must have been like to be a gold miner, ghost stories, school. I listened in amazement as these holy terrors talked about their teachers. It turned out that the one they most admired was the school crank, a tough old cop-on-the-beat who asked no quarter and gave none in his presentation of grammar, Edgar Allan Poe, and difficult vocabulary lists. On the other hand, the "nice" teachers—the ones who never assigned homework, who frequently had "study hall" (another term for a bull session) instead of class, who passed everybody whether they deserved it or not—came in for a hiding. At intimate times like that evening around the campfire one discovers how kids really feel. They just aren't that dumb. Even the baddest of the bad actors knows that teachers who are "nice" to them in school are really killing their chances to make it in the outside world.

Social biologists tell us that when you consider the reproductive life cycle of *Homo sapiens,* we as a species are never more than thirty years or so from the brink of extinction. The analogy to education is clear. Should our schools fail, we are never more than a couple of generations removed from the loss of our loftiest cultural attainments. That's why human beings since the dawn of civilization have worked hard to come up with ways to steep succeeding generations in the wisdom of the collective culture. Given the amount of time and energy that has gone into developing this art, it's not surprising that the great ideas in education have been thoroughly mapped. We can tinker and we can refine and we can adapt. But if we wholesale abandon an approach tempered in the smithy of our experience, we do so only at great peril. What happened in the sixties was that we lost sight of that simple fact. In the face of attacks alleging that our schools were elitist, irrelevant, oppressive, boring, and racist, we forgot the answers.

In this book, I propose to lay those answers out again—to build the case for traditional education from the ground up. Why do we have a public school system in this country instead of leaving it up to free enterprise? What does it take for a democracy to survive? Is there a legitimate public interest in inculcating virtue? These are not new questions, nor are the answers offered here original to me. The best minds attending the birth of our republic struggled with these questions and acted on them. And so must we—or suffer the consequences.

I do not pine with nostalgia for a golden era of education that never transpired. Our public education system has always been imperfect. The criticism of the sixties that it encouraged docility at the expense of curiosity was a telling one, and we should act on it. But it is the nature of a school system that it can always be improved. The trick is to go about that task constructively, encouraging what is healthy and pruning away the deadwood. Innovation is fine, but not for its own sake and certainly not at the expense of programs that work.

You might suppose that traditional education is the sort of apple pie and motherhood idea that no one would oppose—but nothing could be further from the truth. The reform agenda will mean culling several sacred cows from the pedagogical herd, and lately the political sniping against this agenda from entrenched interests has been picking up tempo. The nation's largest teachers' union, for instance, has fought tooth and nail against measures to streamline the firing of incompetents, against merit pay for the best teachers, and against other necessary reforms. Certain civil-liberties purists think that the idea of teaching values in public schools amounts to a confusion of church and state. Some minority spokespersons accuse the excellence in schools movement of harboring a racist motivation in disguise. Die-hard tax revolutionaries say that school reform is fine, as long as it doesn't cost them a cent. And, of course, there's the sheer bureaucratic inertia of such a huge institution.

All in all, the opposition to reform is formidable, but not insurmountable, provided enough people pitch in. Every year the Gallup Poll surveys public opinion about our school system and every year the finding is the same: by a massive majority, U.S. citizens believe that the quality of education we provide our children is more important to our security and future than any other investment, including national defense. I couldn't agree more. But we have to act on that consensus, not just talk about it.

Critics tend to disparage visions of a better future for our schools as pie-in-the-sky "millenial" thinking. But consider this: a child enrolling in first grade in the fall of 1985 will graduate from college in the year 2001. Even by the calendar, that's the next millenium. We have the power to make that child's future very much brighter by rolling up our sleeves now and setting to work, following the master blueprint of a traditional education. Education reform is not an event, it is a process, one that must be sustained over the long haul. To be effective, the cause needs a core of dedicated individuals working toward the same goal. The first step is to become informed. In the next chapter, we begin that journey with the most fundamental question of all: what is the purpose of the public schools?

CHAPTER TWO

The Purpose of School

S CHOOLS are such a universal fact of life these days that we tend to take access to learning for granted. Even among the most poverty-stricken countries on earth, rudimentary school systems extending to the village level have been set up, on the sound assumption that only through literacy will people gain the knowledge they need to help themselves. In historical terms, however, mass education is a fairly recent development. Even as civilized a nation as Great Britain didn't guarantee a high school degree to all its youngsters until after World War II. In the original thirteen colonies, judging by legal documents from the early eighteenth century, two-thirds of the women couldn't even sign their names. Nonetheless, it was in the fledgling United States that the notion that all the people should be schooled first caught on.

The idea of public education is one of this country's distinctive gifts to the modern world. No country ever before tried it on such a massive scale. Today, virtually every nation— communist or capitalist, rich or poor, east or west—does so, to the limits of its wealth or tolerance for free inquiry. Why should this be? Why should an upstart among nations, a country perched on the edge of a raw continent and separated by an ocean from the European intellectual wellspring, have blazed the trail in mass education? The answer to that question reminds us of the special historic mission of schools in a democracy.

The first law requiring instruction in the colonies and appropriating taxes for that purpose was the Massachusetts General School Act of 1647. "It being one chiefe project of the oulde deluder Satan to keep men from the knowledge of the Scriptures," the Puritans declared, "it is therefore ordered that every township after the Lord hath increased them in number to 50 householders, shall appoint one to teache all such children as shall resort to him to write and reade." Plainly, the impulse here was religious. The "hornbook" used to teach reading back then was a little paddlelike affair with the alphabet and numbers inscribed on one side and the Lord's Prayer on the other. In religious intent, then, colonial education resembled its European antecedents, such as the Lutheran vernacular schools of Würrtemberg. It was a means of inculcating the community religion, which, in turn, was a means of establishing a social utopia.

All of that changed with the great burst of creative insight animating the Declaration of Independence and the United States Constitution. Drawing on thinkers of the Enlightenment such as Montesquieu and John Locke, the founding fathers put forward a radical new idea—that government derived its just powers from the consent of the governed (and not the other way around). The people were king. In order to ensure that their consent was not coerced, the various freedoms—of speech, of the press, of assembly, of religion—were guaranteed in the Bill of Rights. And, in order to ensure a fair means of settling controversies, an absolute standard of arbitration was agreed on—majority rule.

We forget what a bold stroke this was. At the time of the Declaration of Independence, the governments of Europe were monarchies or theocracies or some combination of the two. Their underlying premise was that people were inherently weak-willed, ignorant, and susceptible to all manner of folly and therefore required the authority of religion or monarch (who generally claimed a mandate from God, anyway) to curb their baser tendencies. The founding fathers rejected all that. The tyranny of George III had convinced them never to place their trust in a king; and, as descendants of those who had fled the various persecutions of Europe, they weren't about to establish a state religion (even supposing they could have agreed on one).

As a source of authority, that left the people themselves. But were they reliable? The republican form of government, from the time of ancient Rome onward, had a rather disconcerting habit of devolving into either the anarchy of mob rule or the despotism of the dictator. Some feared that a government by the people would be paralyzed by indecision; others, that the majority would prove intolerant and oppress the minority. Thomas Jefferson answered the doubters with a famous rebuttal that remains to this day the bedrock justification for public education in a democracy: "I know no safe depository of the ultimate powers of the society but the people themselves, and if we think them not enlightened enough to exercise their control with a wholesome discretion, the remedy is not to take it from them but to inform their discretion."

When Jefferson wrote these lofty sentiments, "we the people" were a relatively select group of male landowners and taxpayers. It is estimated that at the birth of our nation, only one in fifteen adults had the right to vote. But as the ballot was extended to the rest of the male populace in the nineteenth century and to women in the twentieth, the vast implications of Jefferson's prescription became clear. Public school advocates like Horace Mann, who gave up a promising political career to take a poorly paid job as secretary of the Massachusetts Board of Education, rode from town to town in New England, eloquently urging the case for an expanded public education system. "Ignorance has been well represented under the similitude of a dungeon," Mann used to preach to town meetings, "where, though it is full of life, yet darkness and silence reign. But in our society, the bars and locks have been broken; the dungeon itself is demolished; the prisoners are out. They are in the midst of us. We have no security but to teach and renovate them." The idea was that only education could render the people worthy of the great responsibility accorded them in a democracy. Paying taxes for that purpose was promoted strictly as a matter of enlightened self-interest. "No wonder education so quickly became the American religion," historian Henry Steele Commager has observed. "Education was to be what religion had been in a less secular age—the chief instrument for the regeneration of the human race."

The purpose of the schools was, in short, to elevate the populace. But what exactly did that entail? The Romans had their Law of the Twelve Tablets. Alcuin issued the capitularies under Charlemagne. St. Ignatius of Loyola prescribed the *Ratio Studiorum* for the teaching order of the Jesuits. All in all, over the centuries millions of words have been devoted to how best and to what ends the people were to be elevated. For our purposes, however, we can greatly distill the matter. We start with a simple observation: any school system, no matter the size, must

✳

achieve its goals one student at a time. That is to say, when we discuss the purpose of the U.S. public schools, we are really talking about the effect we wish to have on the individual, multiplied several million times. But when we look at the individual, we find various capacities. As Paul Gagnon has observed, each of us carries within us three discrete social identities: that of the worker, that of the citizen, and that of the private person. The performance of the worker has economic consequences for society; the performance of the citizen collectively determines society's political tone; and the performance of the private person defines the culture. Together, these roles cover a lot of territory. Considering them one at a time, we can arrive at a serviceable understanding of what the schools should strive to accomplish.

Very well then, what about the worker? Few would dispute that a basic function of our school system is to prepare students to enter the working world and to earn a living. In discharging this responsibility, however, the schools must beware of the tactics of the proverbial general who led his troops into battle equipped to win the last war. The job market is, and always has been, a moving target. At the turn of the century, 40 percent of the U.S. labor force worked on farms; today, 3 percent does. And there are equally jarring forces reshaping the economy today. For example, we are entering an increasingly competitive era of international trade rivalry. The backbone of our economy—the automobile industry—was outengineered, undersold, and nearly bankrupted by foreign car makers in the seventies and managed a recent rebound only with the help of "voluntary" trade limits observed by the Japanese. In one industry after another—steel, videocassette recorders, shoes, precision machine tools—we have lost domestic markets (and jobs) to a combination of cheap overseas labor, shrewd capital investment, government subsidies, the overvalued dollar, and, all too frequently, superior product design and manufacture. The lesson here is plain, and we must have the good sense to face it: our schools, which represent the capital investment we make in human productivity, have got to become more rigorous and more committed to excellence (like every other sector of our economy), or we will not be able to maintain our standard of living.

In simple economic terms, there are two reasons why we have to upgrade the level of education we provide our youth to something approaching that of the college bound. First, the job market is changing in a revolutionary way. In 1982 General Motors employed five unskilled workers on its assembly lines for every skilled one. But, to stay competitive with the Japanese, GM has begun investing heavily in robotics, so that by the early nineties the company expects that its ratio of skilled to unskilled workers will be down to a lean and frugal one to one. Nor is this an isolated case. The Bureau of Labor Statistics forecasts that by 1995 about half of all new jobs will require high levels of educational attainment. A full third will be technical, scientific, managerial, or professional. In addition, another 15 to 20 percent of workers—secretaries, nurses, legal assistants, and so forth—will be performing at a significantly more demanding skill level (see Appendix A). As always, the race is to the swift, but more and more in our information-driven society, the jobs will go to the well educated.

Second, and more generally, we have to improve the schools because in the end intelligence is our only edge. No one wants to see U.S. labor working for sweatshop wages. But, as an old blue-collar adage puts it, "From the shoulders down, no man is worth more than a minimum wage." We have to compete with our brains, not our backs. Some of the most promising sectors of our economy—computers and other uses of the integrated circuit, bioengineering, telecommunications, and fiber optics—grew directly out of postwar research and development. But what about the future? Who will win the race to develop the first ceramic internal combustion engine? The "fifth generation" computer with its artificial intelligence capability? the therapeutic "magic bullet" capable of discerning a health cell from a cancerous one and eradicating the latter? These questions are not rhetorical. These races, and others like them, are all real enough and are being run this very moment in the best laboratories and think tanks around the globe. The technological breakthroughs themselves may not even be the deciding factor. The lesson of the recent past seems to be that the society with the collective intelligence to capitalize on them—in other words, with the resourceful work force that can adapt quickly to change—is likely to prosper in the long run. Unfortunately, the hard fact is that, in matters of general education, compared to our trading partners we have been resting on our academic laurels.

Japan provides a good comparison. The school year begins there in the middle of April and ends in late March. Classes are held five days a week from 8:30 in the morning to 3:00 in the afternoon and on Saturday until 12:30. Add these hours up and you discover that, compared to a U.S. student, the average Japanese receives the equivalent of four extra years of schooling by the time he or she graduates from high school. The average high school student in Japan does more homework (two hours on weekdays, three on Sunday) than the top 5 percent of academic performers in the United States do. But it isn't just the total time put in, the schooling is also markedly more demanding. Japanese students take a fixed curriculum of solid academic courses: physics, chemistry, biology, algebra, geometry, calculus, and three years of Japanese literature, of English, and of social studies. In the United States, students choose among a smorgasbord of uneven value. In his excellent book *Japan's High Schools,* Thomas Rohlen presents a fill-in-the-blank section on Greek philosophy from the 1974 Kobe University entrance exam. Among other things, the questions required a working knowledge of the differences among Sophism, Epicureanism, and Stoicism; assumed a command of what Socrates, Plato, and Aristotle stood for; and probed the student's understanding of Phaedrus' famous dictum, "Humans have many ways of measuring things." How would you have scored? Rohlen decided that the Japanese high school diploma was arguably the equivalent of a U.S. bachelor's degree. "I found this conclusion hard to believe at first," he wrote. "But the more I looked at the fundamental facts, the more convinced I became that the majority of high school graduates in Japan would compare well with the majority of our university graduates in terms of basic knowledge in all fields and in mathematics and science skills." And the last sobering piece of news is that the Japanese succeed in leading fully 91 percent of their students through this taxing regimen; with a much less challenging high school curriculum, we graduate only 75 percent of ours.

I don't think for a moment that the Japanese system offers a particulary good model for us to follow: it depends too heavily on the dutiful memorization of facts, on the teacher lecturing and the student passively listening, and on the university entrance exam as the arbiter of all relevance. Nonetheless, we

*

should recognize the considerable accomplishment of our competitor. With a smaller population, the Japanese are turning out more electrical engineers than we are. The silicon chip was invented in the United States, but the Japanese perfected the industrial production of the 64K RAM chip, the memory chip used to store information in computers. As a result, they dominate the market for the integrated circuit, with sales in billions of dollars each year. A juggernaut of an education system made that possible.

We have other competitors besides the Japanese. Economic competition is coming from every direction. And, in standardized achievement tests in mathematics, science, literature, and reading, U.S. students have not been doing well compared to Europeans. In mathematics, for instance, out of twenty nations tested in a 1982 International Educational Achievement study, U.S. eighth graders ended up coming in tenth in arithmetic skills, sixteenth in geometry and eighteenth in measurement. An international standard of excellence in education has been chalked on the wall. If we are to survive as an economic leader, we are going to have to measure up to that mark academically.

Now we turn to the second capacity which a school system is expected to encourage—the student as citizen. One of the proudest chapters in the history of the public schools was written at the beginning of this century when millions of immigrants from eastern and southern Europe streamed to these shores. The public schools taught these children how to speak English, how to read and write, about the history of our democratic institutions, and about the responsibilities of a citizen. In their turn, the immigrants contributed mightily to the building of the nation. Freed from the restraints of class, of ethnic and religious prejudice (comparatively, if not absolutely), they let loose a wave of individual initiative and creative energy across this land. It is no accident that many of the United States' Nobel Prize winners have been second-generation descendants of immigrant families.

As we have already seen, the schools are concerned with raising good citizens in the United States for the familiar Jeffersonian reason: our citizenry must be educated because in a democracy the people make the decisions. But does education still make a difference, with the habit of democracy so firmly rooted in a population some 240 million strong? Unequivocally, yes. For one thing, newcomers continue to arrive. One out of every ten U.S. citizens was born abroad. Today, immigrants are arriving from every land and political tradition; they include Indian Sikhs, Russian Jews, Yorubas from Nigeria, and Mexican peasants. After the Vietnam War, one of the largest groups of Southeast Asian refugees settled in California. Many of these children have excelled in public schools— earning top grades, making the honor roll, being selected as class valedictorians. When it comes to acculturating pupils, the public school magic still works.

The larger point remains to be made, however. And that is, in terms of our democratic institutions, every child in this country is born an immigrant. In essence, we all start out unaware of the uniqueness of our ongoing experiment in self-rule and of the individual's key role in passing that torch to the next generation. Youngsters won't pick up a sense of the grandeur of this undertaking in the way they might pick up a common cold—by casual contact. The schools have to make the case boldly, in terms of information as well as of emotional connection. Part of developing good citizens is simply spreading the lore: what rights are guaranteed under our constitution, what equality under the law means, who does what in our government. But equally important is developing in our children a sense of belonging, a loyalty to our past, and a willingness to participate in our future.

That doesn't mean ignoring those times in our collective past when actions fell short of ideals. The history of this country has its underside; for example, the principle of slave ownership was recognized in the Constitution and it took a civil war to extirpate it. We shouldn't bowdlerize the past, but we shouldn't demean it either. Raising good citizens in a democracy is a balancing act. On one hand, we want to create independent thinkers, people who are well-informed, skilled at asking penetrating questions, and capable of separating the wheat from the chaff and making up their own minds once the facts are in. On the other, we want to inculcate a loyalty for the best in our democratic tradition—for that golden strand of idealism that runs from the Declaration of Independence through the inaugural address of John Kennedy—because schools have a conserving function to perform, too. Our schools must communicate this basic message: in a democracy, no one is let off the hook. Cynicism isn't an excuse for not getting involved. We live in a world where all it takes for evil to triumph is for good people to do nothing. The stakes are high, and we're all responsible.

Right now, we're not even getting across to students the most elementary facts about who we are. I flew to Houston for a conference and caught a taxi into town. The driver, a blonde, pony-tailed extrovert, chattered away from portal to portal; she had just finished high school and this was her first job. When a Honda pulled alongside, she honked and gave the driver the raspberry—she just didn't like those Japanese imports. Was it because the Japanese had fought against us in the war, I wondered? We didn't fight the Japanese, she patiently explained, that was the Vietnamese. No, I said, I meant during World War II. That was against the Germans and Russians, she insisted, we never fought the Japanese.

Ignorance of our recent past is one thing, but the lack of knowledge about basic civics is even more alarming. For instance, in a national test one out of seven seventeen-year-olds agreed with the incredible proposition that the President doesn't have to obey the law; a full 20 percent didn't even know that a Senator is elected.

Even many of our best students seem blissfully unaware of how much a democracy depends on free rational inquiry, a willingness for people to be law abiding and ethical, and disciplined participants in civic affairs. University students who shout down speakers with whom they disagree, or cavalierly sanction getting arrested as a tactic to advance a cause or make a statement, even when the democratic process is open and responding, are planting the seeds of destruction of our freedoms. After all, it was a decade of disorder and mob rule in German universities that helped pave the way for the Nazis. As for emotional connection, the majority in Presidential elections these days is truly silent: most eligible adults don't vote. And the younger the eligible person, the less likely he or she is to do so. We can do better than that in defense of our free society.

The third major purpose of education concerns the cultivation of the private person. Schools should develop the potential skills, abilities, aptitudes, and talents of the student in order to encourage the full flowering of each child's humanity. We speak of a good education having a broadening effect. What we mean

✳

by that is that education expands the students' horizons. It introduces them to the astonishing world found under a microscope, to the crystalline precision of the language of mathematics, to "the best that has been thought and known," as Matthew Arnold put it, in literature, biography, philosophy, and history. An education shows the child heroes and villains, myths and legends, Valley Forge and My Lai, a flat stretch at Kitty Hawk and a wooden tower at Alamogordo. Modest scientists singled out for an award often excuse themselves with a disclaimer: they were standing on the shoulders of their predecessors, they say. But isn't that exactly how we all enlarge our perspectives, by standing on the shoulders of geniuses? by surveying the world from atop the mountain of intellectual and ethical achievements that they have built up over the centuries? We are all heirs to a rich tradition of thought and insight. An education simply makes that heritage available to us. It makes us more powerful by expanding our choices and by putting those choices in a fuller, deeper, and more subtly nuanced frame of reference.

This logic leads us to the brink of a controversy. Because it is concerned with individual choice, education inevitably ends up focusing on the most important questions of all—the ones we carry locked in our hearts. What is a worthwhile goal for the individual to pursue? What does the example of history show us about individual worth? What is the good life? The facile answers—the pursuit of money or power or sensual pleasure—are not enough and have never been enough to satisfy the deepest yearnings of our humanity. Aristotle pointed out that those who had experienced both ways of living, the life of the senses and the virtuous life, generally ended up choosing the latter. Our challenge as educators is to equip students with

enough vistas so that they can make a reasoned choice for themselves. Remember, in classical times, reason didn't connote icy
logic or unrelieved rationality; it meant having enough emotional and intellectual breadth and a firm enough grasp on the
moral and ethical tradition so that one could make mature choices
about life. In our reductively materialistic age, even bringing
up the issue of the moral character of education sounds like
religious proselytizing to some. But standing for core values
has always been at the center of the school experience—even
in the United States. Horace Mann put it this way a century
ago: "When the teacher fails to meet the intellectual wants of
a child, it is the case of asking for bread and receiving a stone;
but when he fails to meet the child's moral wants, it is giving
a serpent." School will always convey a strong ethical message
because it is the primary socializing experience for youngsters.
The question isn't whether public schools will teach morality
but rather what moral tone we will choose to convey. Will it
be a patchwork of conformity stitched together out of the ado-
lescent-peer-group rag bag or the highest ethical principles our
culture embraces and adult society stands for?

During the seventies, the public schools were rebuked rather
stridently for regimenting children into social conformity. Talk
about teaching morality will no doubt fan those old flames, as
will such overtly utilitarian goals as we have outlined for the
schools. Critics may well ask, what about the individual? Isn't
there an inherent conflict between what the individual prefers
and what society demands? And isn't all the rhetoric about the
purposes of the schools just a way of disguising the iron fist in
the velvet glove? I don't think so. In fact, as a look at the three
goals for education suggests, the interest of society and of the

individual are not in conflict so much as they are mutually reinforcing.

For instance, as participants in the economy, most workers want a good, well-paying job, and, statistically, the better one's education, the more likely one will be to find such a spot. Society, for its part, wants general prosperity and the ability to compete in world markets. Once again, the better educated the workers, the more likely that goal is to be realized. (A pair of researchers at the Stanford School of Education, Russell Rumberger and Henry Levin, raised a flap in 1984 with a report that asserted that in the future most new jobs will require no post-secondary schooling and will pay wages significantly lower than the average. Their argument is founded on an analysis of Bureau of Labor Statistics projections. I have responded to it in the Appendix of this book in correspondingly technical terms. Let me just say here that I believe Rumberger and Levin are wrong and that betting on a low-tech future would be foolish, unfair to our children, and dangerous to the economic health of this country.)

A similar community of interest exists concerning the goal of fostering good citizens. The individual values personal freedom; the only framework capable of securing that freedom for everyone is a democracy; and a democracy requires the mass of the citizenry to be elevated, both intellectually and morally, by education. That is the paradox at the center of our way of life. Deep in our historical experience is a commitment to liberty, individuality, personal initiative, and self-reliance—the qualities championed by Thoreau, Emerson, and Whitman. And the education system in this country must stress and transmit our belief in those basic qualities. Nevertheless, although self-interest may work fine as the motive force driving the economy, it is not enough to hold together a society. Liberty must be tempered by a set of cooperative ideals—justice, tolerance, honesty, magnanimity, compassion, the willingness to sacrifice for the common good—if our society is to cohere. The founding fathers appreciated the dilemma. "If there is not virtue among us," Thomas Jefferson wrote, "if there be not good, then there is no form of government that can render us secure." It didn't matter whether people recognized a common set of moral values out of religious conviction, for ethical reasons, or as a political act. The upshot was the same: citizens in a democracy had to accept the responsibility for making a moral effort.

That's the democratic bet. We are the pinnacle of a society dedicated to freedom and individualism and pluralism. But, for such a society to survive, that individualism must be leavened by a sense of responsibility. Take the right to vote. One vote hardly ever makes the difference in an election, and many individuals use this fact to excuse themselves from casting their ballot. But if everyone acted that way, we would lose our democracy. An analogous argument could be made about paying taxes or serving in the military. Enough citizens must pay attention to public affairs and act for the common good if we are to maintain our freedom.

When it comes to education's third goal, that of cultivating the private person, reconciling society's interest with the individual's is a little trickier. For individuals to discover their full humanity, I have argued, their education must include a moral component. The obvious rejoinder is, what's in it for them? Why shouldn't they be allowed to cut every corner possible? After all, *Looking Out For Number One* wasn't a best-selling book because the public despised the idea. Why should the schools purvey an outmoded altruism that will only handicap those gullible enough to fall for it?

The idealistic answer is that a moral life is more fulfilling than a narrow self-absorbed one. The pragmatic answer is that the best way to look out for number one turns out to be looking out for numbers two, three, four, and so on. Take an example as mundane as littering. Someone discards an empty bottle in a park in order to avoid the trouble of finding a trash can. The short-term gain is minimal, as is the apparent damage. But, if littering becomes the norm, the individual only succeeds in making both self and others thoroughly miserable because the park as a place to enjoy a sunny day is spoiled. My point is that there is such a thing as exemplary behavior and such a thing as moral littering. Quite simply, when we are civil—when we show respect, consideration, friendship, or concern for each other—society becomes a more gracious and enjoyable place to live for all of us. When we are generous to the needy, conciliatory in the presence of anger, honest when dishonesty would go undetected, we are helping to create a better world.

I do not contend that such ethical behavior is either easy to live up to or "natural" for any of us, but it is ultimately the most satisfying course of conduct. Becoming moral is an ongoing challenge. It helps put things in perspective to remember that Confucius once wrote, "At seventy, I could follow the desires of my heart without trespassing the right." We are all striving toward that inner harmony of thoughts, wishes, and deeds but attaining it is a lifetime's achievement. That's why schools (and the rest of society's institutions) must uphold, even celebrate, the ideal of the virtuous life—because ethical behavior is learned. The wisdom of the past has the power to help the student see the worthiness of this goal. It can inspire and uplift.

And it plays a crucial part in the child's moral formation. The schools do not bear this burden by themselves, of course. The family and church have primary responsibility to instruct in this area, and they can do so most powerfully by setting a good example. Nonetheless, the schools *do* have an obligation to uphold the core values the student is taught at home. Part of the educational reform movement involves facing up to that challenge once again.

Now we have a good idea of what the public schools are supposed to accomplish, and we can turn to the problem of how to get the job done. In the next chapter, I define what I mean by a traditional education, then describe why it best serves to create that which is desired—the superior worker, the active citizen, and the fulfilled individual.

CHAPTER THREE

The Case for Traditional Education

WHEN I was a sophomore at Stanford University, I caught a ride to Sun Valley with a graduate student to do some skiing over spring break. Little Richard was hot in music back then and Elvis was warning frenzied fans to stay off his blue suede shoes, but during our entire trip this imperturbable fellow kept the radio tuned to classical music: Handel, Mozart, Vivaldi, Dvorak. I ragged him unmercifully. What is this *scratching?* Don't you know which century we're in? My friends decided I lost that bout because when we arrived, the disgusted driver invited me to find another ride home. But, in a larger sense, I won. By the end of that semester, I had started my own classical record collection, and today one of my main sources of recreation is playing the piano.

I sometimes think of this experience when teachers tell me that their students find it "boring" to study the masterworks of literature or the great breakthroughs in science. So what else is new? We should know by now that even when young people end up completely enthralled by a facet of the mature culture, it isn't unusual for them to have been dragged, kicking and screaming, to the initial encounter. The brashness of youth is hardly an infallible guide to the treasure trove of ethical and aesthetic insights available in our heritage. One of the prerequisites of an effective education system is a supreme confidence that—even when the going gets tough—the message being delivered merits the students' time and will richly reward their honest effort. The public schools lost their institutional self-assurance in the seventies. I believe following the precepts of a traditional education is the best way to regain it. In this chapter I examine exactly what is meant by that term and why I believe such an approach best secures a brighter future for our nation and our kids.

What is a traditional education? It can be identified by the following traits. First, and preeminently, a traditional education leads the student through a rigorous curriculum in the academic disciplines—the humanities, natural sciences, and mathematics. It avoids the humbug of allowing adolescents to steer themselves down intellectual blind alleys via such hip, esoteric, or vapid electives as Poetry and Rock, Heroines of the Silent Screen, and Bachelor Survival. Instead, it assumes that educators know what it takes to initiate the child into the intricacies of our civilization and that we have the integrity to insist on nothing less than the best for each student. A traditional education recognizes the value of a student's time on task as well as independent effort and efficiently stretches both by assigning homework every night. Classrooms are orderly and purposeful places; students treat one another with respect, raise their hands when they have something to say, and look up to their teacher as an ambassador of culture from the adult world—not just a pal.

Significantly, a traditional education has high expectations of all parties concerned—students, teachers, parents, and administrators—and holds them accountable. Nothing tells the tale

*

of our schools' retreat from old-fashioned standards of hard work and accomplishment more dramatically than the fact that in the seventies even as national test scores showed student achievement hurtling downward year after year, the average grade on report cards was steadily rising. In the traditional school, students are tested on a regular basis and earn grades commensurate with their effort and performance. Teachers know their subjects and come prepared to class; if they don't the principal replaces them.

In its landmark report, the President's Commission on Excellence in Education focused on the importance of curriculum reform. Its main recommendation was that all students seeking a high school diploma be required to study what it labeled the "Five New Basics": four years of English, three years of mathematics, three years of science, three years of social studies, and a half year of computer science. Certainly, to encourage more students to take such a program would be a step in the right direction. According to the National Center for Education Statistics, if such a set of requirements had been in effect in 1982, only 2.6 percent of the United States' high school seniors would have qualified for graduation.

In California, a Stanford University team looked at the course of studies students had been following through high school and filed its report with the Department of Education in January of 1984. The results of the "Path Study" were eye-opening. The Stanford researchers found that the high school population was, in effect, divided up into four distinct "tracks": the honors track with about 10 percent of all students, the remedial track with 10–15 percent, the college prep track with up to 35 percent, and the biggest group of all, the general track, with around 45 percent. Unfortunately, it was precisely this last and largest group who were following the weakest and most incoherent program. College-bound students have to take a certain number of academic courses to satisfy entrance requirements, but general track students didn't even face this minimal discipline. Of the few courses required by the various California school districts for graduation, a full 42 percent were nonacademic in nature—Physical Education, Consumer Education, Driver's Training. Furthermore, the Path Study found that in contrast with the college prep students the general track students had fewer requirements to fulfill and more electives to choose from and, typically, received no advice from counselors. The result was predictably grim. A sample transcript of a general track student published in the report showed a sprinkling of required civics and language arts classes along with: (as a freshman) Typing, Cultural Awareness, and Homemaking; (as a sophomore) Clothing 2, Beginning Restaurant Management, and Physical Education; (as a junior) Exploring Childhood, Beginning Arts and Crafts, and Cafeteria Aide; and (as a senior) Food for Singles, Beginning Piano, and Teacher's Aide.

In my opinion, this student—and the millions of others like her—are being defrauded of the education they need to make it in our society. One of the most common misconceptions about the excellence in education movement is that it is aimed solely at the high achieving students, at the expense of the rest. Nothing could be further from the truth. As the Stanford Path Study shows, it is the great cross section of average kids currently languishing in the general track who stand to gain the most from curriculum reform. Right now, they are ending up with high school diplomas, but without a worthwhile education. They are not being challenged to do their best. This trivialization of the curriculum must end. Still, simply requiring

✳

all students to sign up for courses labeled English, U.S. History, Algebra, and Biology won't guarantee that they receive the kind of instruction they need either. For curriculum reform to have any meaning, academic rigor must penetrate to the level of the individual classroom. Therefore, let's turn our attention to the core of academic subjects that every student should encounter in high school. Then, let's see how a traditional education handles each and what the implications are for elementary and junior high schools.

English The backbone of the traditional English curriculum is a systematic exposure to the most compelling works in our literary canon, whether they be classic or contemporary, fiction or nonfiction, novels, short stories, poetry, essays, drama, or speeches. Language is learned through imitation. It follows that schools should keep models of excellent writing in front of their students—novels such as Charles Dickens's *Oliver Twist,* Mark Twain's *Huckleberry Finn,* Ivan Turgenev's *Fathers and Sons,* George Orwell's *Animal Farm*—whopping good tales that also happen to be masterpieces of prose style and penetrating insight into the human condition. The great works of literature *are* great because they powerfully transmit significant cultural and ethical ideas about ourselves, our neighbors, and the world around us. More students deserve a chance to read these apotheoses of our culture; in a traditional curriculum, they get it—both through close textual analysis of core works backed up by class discussion and through individual reading programs. In California, for instance, we have developed a list of 400–500 key literary works selected for their exemplary use of language, moral depth, diversity of perspective, and entertainment value. By the time a student graduates, we expect him or her to have read a healthy sampling of this list. Of course, one doesn't commence with James Joyce's *Ulysses* in the fifth grade. In elementary school, the students should acquire the elementary skills: reading fluency, spelling competence, and knowledge of grammar. Even at this early stage, however, an exposure to the best in children's literature, such as Robert Louis Stevenson's *Treasure Island,* Washington Irving's *The Legend of Sleepy Hollow,* and Louisa May Alcott's *Little Women,* is invaluable.

Speech training, vocabulary development with attention to etymology, and a study of correct usage are also important facets of the traditional English curriculum, but the other great preoccupation of the discipline is teaching students to write well. In achieving that end, there is no substitute for practice. Students of English should learn through experience that writing clear and cogent prose isn't a one-shot affair but rather a painstaking process of conceiving fresh ideas, setting them down in draft form, revising the initial effort, and refining it over and over until the final, satisfactory result is obtained.

In fact, this skill is such a critical one that the responsibility for encouraging it falls on the entire faculty. Essays and reports should be a regular feature of history instruction. In science class, students should be expected to hand in written lab reports, anecdotal accounts of their observations, and essay examinations. And, when they do, their papers should be judged on the quality of their prose as well as the content. The English faculty, for its part, should use examples of fine expository writing from other disciplines, Lewis Thomas's *The Medusa and the Snail* from biology, for example, or J. B. S. Haldane's "On Being the Right Size" from mathematics. This is the way a literate generation is formed—by studying the great authors, absorbing their vocabulary and style, pondering the concepts and moral dilemmas embedded in the best works, and analyzing the ideas in coherent written opinions.

History/Social Science We study history partly to learn from the mistakes of the past, partly to gain inspiration, and partly to honor the truth of the old adage "you can't know who you are until you know whence you came." Modern social studies guides like to rearrange the world for scholarly consumption according to grand, overarching themes, for example, "human conflict," "cultural interaction," and "global understanding," whose loftiness is rivaled only by their ambiguity. The traditional approach is much more down to earth. It tells the story of the memorable people and events of our past and thereby puts students in touch with something quite precious—their heritage. The master organizing principle of a good history course is chronological order. Students are expected to learn about the important themes, incidents, ideas, and personalities of our past. That is, who did what to whom, when, and why? This narrative approach shouldn't be the excuse for a stale recitation of dates and places. On the contrary, because history is about the risk and daring of real people—Hannibal crossing the Alps, Galileo facing the ecclesiastical courts, Eleanor Roosevelt confronting the bonus marchers—it has a unique ability to engage students in the dramatic unfolding of events. And, because it is centrally concerned with questions of meaning and value, it can inspire them to reflect on their own responsibilities. In the traditional history curriculum, students are expected to sharpen their critical intelligence, to debate the momentous issues in class discussions, to sift information and compare points of view, and to come to their own conclusions in frequent written reports and papers.

In terms of content, every high school student should take a year of United States history and geography and a year of world history with an emphasis on Western civilization and an exposure to the diverse stories and histories of other cultures. The U.S. history course should treat both political and social history and cover the major eras, personalities, ideas, and groups that contributed to the building of this nation. Special attention should be paid to the key documents and writings that form the basis of our democracy: the Declaration of Independence, the Federalist Papers, the Constitution, and the Bill of Rights. Students should get to know certain exemplars of the American character: for religious spirit, John Winthrop; for humanitarian concern, Jane Addams; for moral courage, Martin Luther King. To know such heroic figures is to admire them, and to admire them is to wish to become like them in moral stature and purpose. Of course, we have had our share of dark moments in our past—the "Trail of Tears" of the Cherokee, the internment of Japanese-Americans during World War II, the anticommunist witch hunts and blacklisting of the fifties. These failings should be examined, but not to the exclusion of our achievements—the protection of individual freedom, the increase in material well-being, the abiding promise of opportunity for all.

World history and geography portrays the origins of society from the hunter-gatherers to the agricultural revolution and the emergence of the city. In this course, particular attention should be paid to the development of Western civilization, beginning with the rise of democracy in Greek city-states, and the Roman Empire and continuing through the Renaissance, the Reformation, and the Industrial Revolution. Key turning points that have shaped that modern world—the Bolshevik takeover in the Russian Revolution, the decline of colonial rule, the rise of scientific rationalism—should also be investigated. Students should also gain some grasp of the nature and historical experience of the variety of cultures and countries which comprise this globe.

In California, we suggest that a third year of high school social science be devoted to one semester of civics and one semester of economics. The civics course explores the concept of freedom, equality, and community; the democratic rationale; how our local and national government works; and the duties and privileges of the individual citizen. It should give our students an understanding of the fragility of our freedom, and it should also give examples of how life is in countries that don't live by a democratic ethos. The economics course focuses on the nature of our modified capitalist system, the role of private ownership, investment competition, market forces, consumer choice in allocating resources, and the performance of our system as compared with that of centrally managed ones.

Mathematics Mathematics is a language—the language of science—and a powerful means of interpreting the phenomenal world with ideal precision. Mathematics, according to one of its most brilliant exponents, Bertrand Russell, possesses "not only truth, but beauty—a beauty cold and austere, like that of sculpture." We should help students sense the elegance in mathematical systems. It used to be that only those interested in premed, engineering, or the sciences took three years of math in high school. Today, math is integral to nearly every line of work—from the farmer determining what mix of crops to grow next spring to the urban planner predicting the rush-hour transportation load fifteen years in the future or the laid-off factory worker training for a new job.

The traditional math program is sequential, linear, and properly demanding. In elementary school, students learn the fundamentals of arithmetic: how to add, subtract, multiply, and divide with whole numbers, with fractions and decimals, ratios, proportions, percents, roots and powers; and how to solve story problems using these operations. Also presented are some basic properties of figures (such as the Pythagorean theorem), computations of the mean, median, and mode of a set of data, and simple exercises in logic. Compared to other nations, our students tackle these subjects at a much slower pace. In high school, algebra and geometry are studied in depth, along with the concepts of probability and statistics. Students planning to attend college should take advanced algebra and functions as well, and those with aptitude should go on to trigonometry and calculus.

Because the math curriculum builds on itself, it is critically important that students have a firm foundation. Passing a confused or ill-prepared math student to the next level merely creates an impossible situation for the next year's instructor. For this reason, there can be no social promotions in the traditional math setting. On the other hand, high schools can, and should, keep a student's options open. A freshman who is not prepared to take algebra in the ninth grade should have the alternative of entering the college prep sequence in the tenth or eleventh grade after a year or two or boning up.

One final point about beginning math instruction. You can't develop a math sense in students by constant reliance on work sheets. In a recent California achievement test, a third of the sixth graders who missed a question about the height of a horse calculated it was 16 inches tall; another third said 64 feet. Obviously, numbers didn't mean anything to these students. Proper math instruction stresses the real world meaning of numbers by giving students plenty of real world number tasks.

Science   The study of the natural world has furnished us with the technological means to build the wealthiest society in history. But science is also rewarding in its own right. The intellectual challenge of practicing good science—the thrill of the hunt, if you will—is every bit as stimulating and creative as the composition of a symphony or novel. It is this sense of adventure, of discovering the hidden patterns of order in the universe, which a traditional science education tries to arouse. Toward that end, not all science courses are created equal; some have too narrow a focus to orient the beginner. In its analysis of high school transcripts, the National Center for Education Statistics identified thirty-five distinct physical science course titles and thirty-two life science ones, including Rocketry, Acoustics, Pathology, and Biopsychology. These courses may have their place but, in general, a traditional education gives priority to a solid grounding in the essential three: biology, chemistry, and physics. Biology explains the cellular basis of living things, genetics, evolution, principles of classification, ecology, and animal behavior. In chemistry, the atomic structure of matter is studied, along with chemical bonding, the periodic table, acid-base and oxidation-reduction reactions, and the properties of the elements. The physics student learns the laws of mechanics, optics, wave phenomena, electricity and magnetism, the kinetic theory, and the theory of relativity. Together, these three subjects guarantee that students have a good sense of the underlying principles governing the natural world. In addition, in each of the branches of science, the history of the major discoveries should be retraced, through readings (*The Double Helix* by James Watson, for example, is a fascinating account of the discovery of the structure of DNA) or by repeating the results in the lab. In this way, the student gains an insight into how a scientist proceeds; from tentative hypothesis to hypothesis, always skeptical, testing theory against facts, and valuing discovery of the objective truth above all else.

The biology/chemistry/physics sequence is appropriate for the college bound. A less rigorous survey curriculum—perhaps a life science/physical science/earth science sequence—could get across the same basic insights to the general track student without the intimidating technical detail. The important thing is that every student needs to become scientifically literate—and the only way that can be accomplished is by studying science.

Proficiency in a Second Language The study of foreign languages, modern or classical, has reached a distressing state in U.S. schools. In 1970, 23 percent of high school students were enrolled in the study of a foreign language. That figure was disappointing in itself, but by 1980 it had dwindled to a meager 15 percent and most of that number were introductory students in French, German, or Spanish who were likely to drop out after the first year. This record is unacceptable. It takes a minimum of four to six years in most academic settings to gain a passing command of a second language, that is, the ability to maintain a conversation, read some literature, and write reasonably coherent paragraphs. In the traditional education scheme, every child—not just a handful—would develop such a capacity. One might ask, why should they when English has become the *lingua franca* of the twentieth century? One answer is that a foreign language can be useful in itself—when traveling or fol-

✳

lowing a career in trade, diplomacy, law, science, or the arts. Also, learning a second language is one of the very best ways to improve language sense in general, including one's command of the mother tongue. The common roots of words, the protean nature of grammar, the intimate connection between language and thought—a host of valuable insights accrue to the foreign language student. And finally, in a small world rent by bitter jealousies, the study of a second language is a valuable bridge to understanding, one every student should undertake to build.

Fine or Performing Arts Experience   Music, dance, and the visual arts transcend language to express the continuum of human experience in sound, motion, and image. Together with theatre, these artistic forms have been the vehicles for some of our most profound statements of cultural values. We expect to be challenged, entertained, and sometimes disturbed by art, but we respond to it more confidently when we have some direct knowledge of what is entailed in creating it. Just as the study of biology requires laboratory work to deepen understanding, so opening oneself up to art involves experiencing it firsthand. Consequently, every student should participate in a fine or performing arts project in the course of a traditional education.

Health and Physical Education   Juvenal left off flaying the conscience of the Empire long enough to advise Roman citizens to pray for *mens sana in corpore sano*—a sound mind in a sound body. The traditional education ideal holds good health and mental vigor to be intertwined. Surprising as it may seem in this era of jogging, swimming, aerobics, and fitness, the present cohort of students, kindergarten through twelfth grade collec-

tively, is in atrocious physical shape. On objective measure-
ments of endurance and strength, they perform less well than
did the children of the baby boom. They exercise less and eat
more junk food than they should. In the traditional cirruculum,
each class of students is expected to participate in a program of
regular, supervised, and strenuous exercise. Coordination, dex-
terity, strength, and stamina develop in a predictable order in
children, and excellent sports and athletic programs have been
devised to aid their growth beginning in the elementary grades.

In addition, at some time during the junior high school years,
students should take a health unit under the tutelage of a teacher
trained in the area. Pragmatic Ben Franklin wrote that an ounce
of prevention is worth a pound of cure. With the nation's health
bill soaring, the information dispensed in health classes—on
alcohol and drug abuse, nutrition and diet, first aid, common
communicable diseases and preventive health care, sex education, and mental health—could well save more needless misery,
suffering, and expense than any other course in the curriculum.

And there you have it: English, history, a foreign language,
mathematics, science, the fine arts, and health and physical education is the irreducible core of the modern traditional education. It's the best preparation for life money can buy. Look
at the most prestigious (and expensive) preparatory schools in
the United States, places like Exeter, Andover, and Choate,
which send hundreds of alumni to Ivy League colleges every
year. These schools train the children of the leaders in commerce and industry. What course of studies do they offer? It
won't surprise you to learn that, essentially, it's the traditional

curriculum I have just described. They rely on this demanding formula because it has proven that it works. My position is that if it's good enough for the sons and daughters of the nation's leaders, then the children of the middle class and of those striving to escape poverty deserve no less.

What explains the effectiveness of the discipline-based approach? Or, in other words, why does a traditional education work? Now that we know what is meant by the term, we can address this important question in the remainder of this chapter.

Let's begin with a closer look at the nature of the problem. High school achievement scores have dropped over the last twenty years, it's true—but not uniformly. In fact, the lowest quartile of SAT test-takers has actually been doing better over the last decade. Meanwhile, the SAT scores of the most talented have been in a swoon. From 1972 to 1981, the proportion of test-takers scoring in the 600–800 range fell from 11.4 percent to 7 percent on the verbal and from 17.8 percent to 14.5 percent on the math. The conclusion is that it's the decrease in the ranks of the high achievers, particularly in language ability, that has depressed the national SAT results. Why has this happened? To score 600 or better on the SAT, you have to have what educators call "higher-order" learning skills: the ability to analyze complex relationships, to draw inferences, and to reason deductively and inductively. In other words, the problem is that too few of our students know how to think.

This picture is reinforced by data from the National Assessment of Educational Performance. In 1983, the NAEP reported that the so-called "lower-order" learning skills were well in hand at both the elementary and high school levels. "Results for numerical computation, literal reading comprehension and writing mechanics have not wavered appreciably over the past decade," it said. On the other hand, the higher-order cognitive skills—math problem solving, complex writing tasks, and inferential reading comprehension—were continuing to fall. It is this convergence of student performance at the level of the barely tolerable that the President's Commission aptly described as the "rising tide of mediocrity" in our schools.

As a case study of what's causing that rising tide, take the issue of literacy. Jeanne Chall, a professor of education at Harvard University and one of the country's leading experts in reading, summarized the important trends in her recent book *Stages of Reading Development*. Reading skills in children develop in three stages: code-breaking (kindergarten and first grade), reading for fluency (second and third grade), and reading to learn (fourth and higher grades). Chall cites evidence to show that the schools are succeeding for the most part in the early stages, that is, in teaching the mechanical skills of decoding and fluency. But they are falling down in the upper elementary grades when reading becomes the means of acquiring new information. For example, in nationwide tests of reading, writing, and vocabulary, low-income and minority students score just as well as middle-class children in the first, second, and third grades. In fourth grade, however, their scores begin to slip; by sixth grade, a considerable gap separates them and continues to widen through high school. What explains this disheartening pattern?

The obvious answer is that a high level of literacy involves more than mastering reading technique; literacy is inextricably linked to content. To be sure, skills of decoding and fluency are a necessary condition of learning to read, but they are not sufficient. Reading ability also depends on how much you already know about the subject. This point was brilliantly illus-

✳

trated in a series of experiments by E. D. Hirsch, Jr. of the University of Virginia. Hirsch administered reading and writing exams to a group of students selected from a variety of cultural backgrounds. It turned out that when the reading matter or writing topic was familiar to the students, their reading comprehension and writing skills in all dimensions improved markedly. For example, U.S. students born in this country always scored better after reading accounts of a traditional Protestant or Catholic wedding than they did after reading about a Hindu ceremony, and students from the subcontinent of India scored in just the opposite pattern. Clearly, the reading matter hadn't changed nor had the technical reading skills of the students. What did change was the amount of relevant prior knowledge that the test-takers had, and this determined their comprehension level. Literacy, in short, is not an empty form or skill; it also depends on how much you already know about what's being read.

All of this has extraordinary implications for how we teach. The inference from the new understanding of literacy is that any knowledge a child might acquire could eventually help that child understand some text or another. To build up literacy, then, it follows that one important step is constantly to present significant, new information to students and continually to open up new frontiers of knowledge on which children can exercise their growing linguistic abilities. Hirsch uses the term "cultural literacy" to describe this crucial fund of socially enabling knowledge and argues that expanding it is a key function of the schools.

Unfortunately, we have been doing just the opposite. Children need an orienting core of knowledge about their social, political, and moral worlds, but we have been emptying the curriculum of all content. The Achilles heel of our instructional program is the upper elementary grades. Research shows that that is when children are the most naturally curious. That's when we should be shifting from a narrow skill-based curriculum to the study of literature, science, and history to excite students. Children need informative reading material to sustain their interest, but we have been giving them textbooks gutted of all substance and pitched to an illusory least common denominator. Jeanne Chall found a startling association between textbook series and the SAT scores of students who used them: the harder the series, the higher the SAT scores. Learning is seamless and nothing is wasted. Is it any wonder that so little has been coming out of the typical curriculum when so little has been put in?

Returning to the original question—why does traditional education work?—I'm now prepared to venture an answer. A traditional curriculum succeeds where less rigorous approaches fail because it stresses active language mastery, which is the key to clear thinking; because it lays a broad foundation of learning, which provides the necessary information base; and because it engages the whole student, emotions and intellect, which integrates the individual into the common culture.

If the course of studies I have outlined has a theme, it is the central importance of active language mastery. "Reading maketh a full man, conference a ready man and writing an exact man," Sir Francis Bacon declared four centuries ago and his familiar epigram still holds true. The traditional curriculum sets students the task of reading the best literature, discussing issues in class, and writing essays and exam answers. The common denominator in all this is the constant manipulation and active use of English. This emphasis makes sense because language is the medium of the mind. An individual with a rudimentary vocabulary is as poorly equipped to think clearly as a musician with water glasses and a spoon would be to play Brandenburg Concerti. Writing, in particular, exercises the intellect. It forces students to find the words that most persuasively express a point of view and, in the process, wonderfully clarifies the usual muddle. The habit of good writing—the organization of ideas, the marshaling of evidence, the proper choice of words—is virtually indistinguishable from clear thinking. But isn't clear thinking just another name for what educators call the "higher-order" learning skills? It is, and that's why the traditional approach succeeds at developing cognitive capacities while less arduous curriculums do not come close.

It isn't just that the traditional curriculum improves the power of self-expression, however. It also furnishes students with the raw material about which it is worth expressing themselves. It provides a broad foundation of learning so that students are brought into contact with the main ideas of the essential disciplines, those ideas that when mastered enable the student to learn all the others. Thus, a traditional curriculum prepares the way for a lifetime of learning. Some may see the large number of required courses I have outlined here as more of a vice than a virtue, as unnecessarily restrictive of the student's freedom of choice. I disagree. For one thing, such a curriculum still leaves nearly a quarter of the student's schedule open for electives— far more than in Japan. More importantly, though, we should keep in mind what we are up to. If students are bound for college, they will have ample opportunity to pursue their particular intellectual interests there. If they are not, then high school is our last opportunity to convey to them the adult message of what our society stands for—and as a result, we have all the more reason to make careful use of the time. It is a peculiar definition of freedom that would conform our curricula to the intellectual aspirations of adolescents, individuals who are in no position to know the range of opportunities that their choices may be foreclosing. If we believe in the value of education, then we owe each child access to nothing less than the best.

Finally, the traditional curriculum is effective because it reaches the whole student, intellect and emotions. I still remember hearing in the sixth grade about Cincinnatus, the general who came out of retirement to save Rome and then returned to his farm instead of accepting the office of dictator. That sort of story makes a tremendous impression on children. You can't hear it without thinking about what really matters in life. The examples of the past and the memorable stories of literature have almost the force of parable when they are retold in school. They work on several levels: as entertainment, as examples of superb language craft, as psychological primers, as catalysts to thinking about the big issues. They are part of our tribal knowledge. They express our deepest values and beliefs and consequently have great power. A curriculum that omits them is missing what the public schools are all about.

The claim of this book is that a traditional education will give all students the best start in life. In Chapter Two, we agreed on a standard against which we could measure the desirability of any curriculum: does it produce superior workers? active citizens? fulfilled individuals? Let's see how the traditional curriculum measures up, *vis-à-vis* the competition, to the purposes of the public school system we have already identified.

With regard to the goal of developing workers, the alternative to the traditional curriculum has always been vocational education. Vocational education is the "hands-on" approach to learning. Students who, because of their temperament or perceived lack of intelligence, are unable to keep up with the academic curriculum have routinely been routed to this course of studies. This meant they might spend over half of their high school career in craft-type courses, learning how to make furniture, to sew, to type, to tune a car, or to operate a lathe. Does this kind of training prepare a student to go out and succeed in the world of work? Narrowly conceived of in this way, it does not.

The problem with many vocational education programs is that they are constantly fighting a losing battle with job obsolescence. Welding is a nice skill but less sought after than it used to be: robots are taking over on the production line. The average high school shop with its quaint complement of drill presses, metal lathes, and grinders resembles nothing so much as an industrial museum. The modern machine shop uses "numerically controlled" tools run by computer to cut, drill, mill, and bore materials. You won't find students in many high schools learning to operate these state-of-the-art tools, however. They cost too much.

The idea behind vocational education is that we can teach a set of procedures—how to plumb a house, manage a herd of milk cows, or cook in an institution—that will earn the student's daily bread through a lifetime of productive work. But the pace of technological change is so rapid and pervasive these days that hardly any skill is likely to stay in demand that long. In fact, the average worker can expect to go through five career changes in the course of adult life. That's why the traditional education approach makes more sense. It isn't familiarity with how to run a particular machine that will guarantee employment in the future. What will are the broad, generalizable skills such as the ability to think, plan, and adapt to change, as well as the qualities of initiative, perseverance, and good judgment. That's why I maintain that a traditional education is really the best vocational education around. Employers understand this. Recently, the U.S. Chamber of Commerce, which used to support vocational education aggressively, has come out in favor of a solid core of academic study for all students.

My own view is that, properly structured, vocational education has a helpful role to play in high school education. First of all, we should recognize that it is a supplement, not a substitute, for the core curriculum. That much having been said, however, experience shows that a segment of the student population thrives on applied courses such as Accounting or Keyboarding. These courses can be excellent ways to reinforce the lessons from the academic curriculum by demonstrating the utility of the math operations or writing skills students have been learning. Good vocational education schools have their own standards of excellence and high expectations. At New York City's Aviation High School students have an enthusiasm for what they are learning and a sense of purpose that carries over to the academic courses that are a required part of the curriculum. For the public high school in general, however, vocational education programs should focus on broadly applicable job skills such as typing, computer operation, and mechanical drawing. Training for particular industrial tasks should be left up to places with the budget and expertise to do it right—which means, as a rule, post–high school technical institutes and trade schools.

How to achieve the second purpose of the schools—building

good citizens—is not a subject of hot debate. Practically everyone agrees that you start off by requiring a good, searching course in U.S. history. But you can't stop there. The rest of the humanities curriculum has an equally important role to play. The study of our country's history teaches students the rights and responsibilities of citizenship and fosters an attachment to the high ideals on which this nation was founded. However, education in a free, self-governing society has another duty to discharge. If freedom here is to have any meaning, the schools must also encourage in their young citizens an independent habit of mind.

Consider how schools function in a totalitarian state. In the Soviet Union, science and mathematics are staples of the curriculum. But those subjects that raise first principles—notably literature and history—are rigidly controlled. Only those creative works that reflect the Communist Party's ideological viewpoint are studied in literature class. In history, students learn not only the Party's selective version of what happened in the past, but also its dogmatic analysis of what those events signify. This isn't education as we understand it; it is indoctrination. The student's assent is taken for granted or coerced, not earned by rational means. In a democracy, on the other hand, the whole point is to nurture individuals so that they are capable of reaching an informed judgment. Students are expected to approach issues in a critical, questioning spirit. As their fund of knowledge increases, they begin to make up their own minds on matters of controversy.

By its very nature, the traditional curriculum in the humanities helps form independent thinkers. Every imaginable perspective can be found in our free market of ideas. The only "censorship" that takes place in the traditional curriculum is aesthetic, not ideological. Furthermore, the emphasis on language mastery is also significant. George Orwell believed that totalitarian societies would be required to corrupt daily language—an idea embodied by the Doublespeak of *1984*—in order to disguise the massive hypocrisies inherent in keeping such regimes afloat. To the extent that our own leaders venture into policies of marginal validity, we hear it in their anesthetizing euphemisms. One thinks of such recent lalapaloozas as the doctrine of "anticipatory retaliation" against terrorism or "constructive engagement" in apartheid South Africa. A well-educated populace is less vulnerable to this brand of obfuscation and as a result makes better citizens.

The third purpose of schools concerns the private person. We decided in Chapter Two that school should encourage the full flowering of each student's humanity—in intellect, in health, in aesthetic sensibility, and in character. As I have already shown, the dense matrix of academic, sports, and art programs in the traditional curriculum directly addresses the first three concerns and does so in a much more systematic and organized fashion than does the usual general track curriculum. What I would like to dwell on here is the final aspect, that of character formation.

It's sad to say, but a classical education is no guarantee that its recipient will turn out to be a paragon of virtue. Nazi Germany gave us the monstrous example of Dr. Josef Mengele who oversaw sadistic medical experiments by day and listened to classical music at night. In fact, the world has seen its share of beautifully cultured scoundrels, dissolutes, and ne'er-do-wells. Nevertheless, when it comes to infusing individuals with a sense of moral responsibility, I am prepared to argue that the odds favor the traditional curriculum over any other form of schooling short of the monastery.

✳

How so? Ethical behavior is not a discrete subject in a traditional education; rather, it's the basis for the whole curriculum. A central tenet of our heritage is the importance of individual responsibility. Take a subject like history. The student reads about the events of the past, for example, the smuggling of slaves to freedom via the Underground Railroad before the outbreak of the Civil War. This story has its heroes (among them, crusading editor Frederick Douglass and daredevil Harriet Tubman) and its villains (the bounty hunters and the politicians like John Calhoun who eloquently defended the institution of slavery). It also has a host of important moral implications: that life is more important than property, that every human being has an intrinsic dignity, that there are times when the law *should* be disobeyed. That's quite a lesson for a public school system to be teaching its youth—but we do it every day. All things being equal, I believe students will tend to imitate those individuals whom history celebrates as praiseworthy. Even if they don't, at least they get a better sense of the shared values our society stands for.

The study of English literature broadens the moral perspective of the reader in a similar way. When reading, the student is invited to travel through other places and other times and to see the world through the eyes of another person. That's a big step. At the heart of most ethical systems is the notion of mutuality. The Golden Rule ("Do unto others as you would have them do unto you") and Kant's universalizability principle are two formulations consistent with this principle. For mutuality to work, however, the individual must feel connected to the larger human community. Great literature can create that sense of empathy, of shared vaules, of belonging to a civilization with a common history and common concerns. It may not make us moral—nothing can for certain as long as we have free will—but it does have the power to show us what moral and immoral characters look like. With such a beginning, we may indeed be inspired to emulate the good. Ultimately, however, all that the traditional curriculum makes absolutely certain of is that students will be confronted with the important questions in life. How they answer them is, and must remain, up to them.

To sum up, let me quote from U.S. Secretary of Education William Bennett's speech to the National Press Club, where he captures with felicity the spirit of what our children should learn:

> "It is important to know what justice is and it is important to know what courage is. It is important to know what is noble and what is base. It is important to know what deserves to be defended, and what deserves to be loved. In the words of Montaigne, it is important to know the difference between ambition and greed, the difference between loyalty and servitude, and between liberty and license.
>
> And more. We should want every student to know how mountains are made, and that for most actions there is an equal and opposite reaction. They should know who said, "I am the state" and who said, "I have a dream." They should know about subjects and predicates, about isosceles triangles and ellipses. They should know where the Amazon flows, and what the First Amendment means. They should know about the Donner Party and slavery, and Shylock, Hercules, and Abigail Adams, where Ethiopia is, and why there is a Berlin Wall.

They should know a little of how a poem works, how a plant works, and what "If wishes were horses, beggars would ride" means. They should know the place of the Milky Way and DNA in the unfolding of the universe. They should know something about the Convention of 1787 and about the conventions of good behavior. They should know a little of what the Sistine Chapel looks like and what great music sounds like.

Our students should know our nation's ideals and aspirations. What are they? Well, we the people, all of us, believe in liberty and equality, we believe in limited government and in the betterment of the human condition. These truths underlie our society, and though they may be self-evident, they are not spontaneously apprehended by the young. Our students should know of these ideals, and they should know that a large part of the world thinks and acts according to other beliefs."

I have been writing about an ideal curriculum in an ideal world in this chapter, but I honestly believe that the traditional approach has the most to offer our children. There are those who disagree, however, and in the next chapter, I consider the merits of one of the most potentially damaging arguments against the excellence in schools movement—that it is unfair to children from minority and low-income families.

CHAPTER FOUR

The Excellence Movement and Minority Aspirations

I'LL NEVER FORGET the evening I discovered firsthand how the black intelligentsia views the public schools. Nancy and I had been invited to a dinner party at the Oakland home of our son's pediatrician, Dr. Michael LeNoir. Dr. LeNoir is black, as were most of his guests, a high-powered circle of Bay Area attorneys, doctors, and business professionals, maybe forty people in all. At the time, I was still a member of the state board of education and tended to talk, and ask, about the public schools incessantly. This penchant must have made me a big bore at the party because, as I eventually found out, none of the other couples present had sent their children to public schools. Not one!

Michael LeNoir explained the situation to me later on. It wasn't that he or other leading blacks were philosophically opposed to public education. "Look," he told me, "a lot of my friends went through segregated public school systems in the South. I came from Dallas. It was a no-nonsense, no-frills place. The teachers were black, they taught the basics, they gave us homework, and they expected us to achieve." But that was yesterday's public schools. Today's version, it seems, just isn't tough enough to satisfy these ambitious parents. "Our only avenue of upward mobility was a good education," LeNoir told me, "and we took it. I would *never* allow my children to end up in one of today's lenient schools."

The situation is rich with irony. The desegregation of this country's public schools is rightly regarded as one of our society's major steps forward in this century. From compensatory education money for inner city schools to busing programs, billions of dollars have been spent to put teeth in the Supreme Court's landmark *Brown* v. *Topeka Board of Education* decision. But today, some thirty years after that decision, many black parents have less confidence in the public schools than they did back in the bad old days. Ruby Bridges, who in 1960 was the first black child to crack the race barrier in New Orleans's public schools, recently took her own children out of that system and put them in a parochial school. The point is that desegregation doesn't mean much to parents if the socially enlightened modern school their children are now entitled to attend is shirking its academic responsibilities.

The disenchantment is widespread. The Gallup Poll now shows that about half of all people in this country favor the idea of allowing parents to send their children to a public, private, or parochial school of their choice, using tax-funded vouchers. And among blacks, a whopping 63 percent support the voucher idea. In fact, black parents who really can't afford to, but who see their children trapped in an education system that aims too low, have been setting up their own low-budget, high-expectation schools. According to the National Center for Neighborhood Enterprise, some 250 such independent, minority-run schools are now operating.

The reason for all the discontent is manifest: our public schools have been underperforming in general and failing to educate minority students in particular. Overall, about 13 percent of today's youth are functionally illiterate, but among black males, that figure soars to over 40 percent. A combined math and verbal score of 700 on the SAT is only slightly better than the score that someone marking their answer sheet at random would be likely to achieve. In 1982, 14 percent of white students failed to reach this mark, 27 percent of Hispanics were similarly lagging, but a full 49 percent of blacks couldn't cross this minimum threshold. Obviously, the black community has every reason to be irate over these results. They translate into a lifetime of unemployment, poverty, drugs, crime, and a perpetuation of the cycle of despair. We cannot allow another generation of minority youth to go through school and never receive an education.

Such a squandering of human potential cannot be tolerated because it is so unnecessary. Inner city schools don't have to be breeding grounds for educational failure and social miasma History shows us—and recent experience reinforces the lesson—that given the sound approach of a traditional education, black students can flourish with the same enthusiasm for learning and academic distinction as their white counterparts. I know this from personal experience, but it has been amply documented elsewhere. Writing in the quarterly periodical *The Public Interest,* Thomas Sowell has profiled examples of black excellence in education. Consider the case of Dunbar High School in Washington, D.C.

Dunbar was founded in the basement of a community church in 1870. Its curriculum emphasized the traditional academic disciplines—literature, history, mathematics, sciences, and classical languages—and its students looked at education as an opportunity to get ahead. By the turn of the century, Dunbar had been incorporated into the capitol's public school system and, with its all-black student body and staff, was regularly outscoring white competitors in citywide tests. In fact, over the next half century, graduates of Dunbar High School included the nation's first black general (Benjamin O. Davis), first black federal judge (William H. Hastee), first black Cabinet member (Robert C. Weaver), first black Senator since reconstruction (Edward W. Brooke), and the discoverer of blood plasma (Charles Drew). This record of achievement is all the more notable when you consider the circumstances. Dunbar was never a wealthy institution nor a particularly exclusive one. In its heyday its students were by and large the children of maids and messengers and low-level government clerks. Like most black schools in segregated education systems, Dunbar had to make do with what resources were left over after the white schools had been taken care of. Forty students to a class was commonplace, the blackboards were "crackled like maps," and there never was a public address system.

Still, despite all this adversity, Dunbar was rich in those attributes that matter most. It had a clear bead on the target of academic learning; it had a series of outstanding principals who recruited dedicated teachers and who enjoyed tremendous parental support; it insisted on an orderly atmosphere for learning; and, most of all, it held out high hopes tp and expected a peak performance from every child who came through its doors. The school motto, penned by black poet Paul Laurence Dunbar and inscribed over the auditorium arch, summed up its spirit of self-help and purposeful industry. "Keep on pluggin' away," it read, "Perseverance still is king."

As Sowell records, Dunbar's identity was effectively demol-

✳

ished by the way in which the District of Columbia school board chose to comply with the Supreme Court's desegregation ruling in the mid-fifties. But the spirit of Dunbar High School lives on, for example, schools like Bret Harte Preparatory Intermediate School in Los Angeles which is a few blocks from Watts and a beehive of academic activity. Bret Harte students have homework assignments every night and every weekend, receive weekly report cards, and take three full years of sciences. Students who receive D grades or worse make up the work in summer school. Or take as another example Beasley Academic Center in Chicago, most of whose students come from the adjoining Robert Taylor Hones housing project. Beasley boasts a 95 percent attendance rate and a reading achievement level significantly higher than the citywide average. And then there's half-white, half-minority Edward R. Murrow High School in Brooklyn, where each year 9500 students apply for 800 places. Sixty-five percent of the students at Murrow finish a third year of foreign language and enrollment rates in algebra, geometry, and science compare favorably with those of private prep schools.

It's not that we don't know how to educate black, Hispanic, or other minority youth. What has been missing is the will, or the courage, to do it the right way. Time and time again, two arguments in particular have been raised against the traditional academic approach for minorities, and until recently they have carried the day in public education. I would like to confront these two arguments head on in the next few pages because I believe that, however benign their inspiration or intent, they have done more to prevent the advancement of blacks in our society than have all the fellows in white sheets and pointy hoods.

The first argument against traditional education for minorities is a bit of social paternalism. A proponent of this position might argue as follows: "Academic rigor is fine for college-bound youth, but the average minority youngster just won't be able to handle such a demanding curriculum. Ghetto kids will be turned off by the fancy words and highbrow concerns of another place and time. School has to be relevant and entertaining to hold the attention of youngsters raised on a diet of TV programs. First, they'll be embarrassed by their inability to handle academic courses; then, they'll become hostile to the whole process and get out of control. Vandalism will increase and the dropout rate will soar."

Instead of breaking the child's spirit on the rack of academic excellence, so this point of view argues, the modern curriculum should offer courses in which the average student can succeed: Driver Education, Basic Communications, Team Sports. The student gets an A, feels the flush of self-worth, and goes out into the world with a positive self-image.

What's wrong with this picture? It faithfully mirrors the prevailing mind-set of many public schools over the last two decades. Unfortunately, what it doesn't reflect is something far more important—reality. For example, we are told that the traditional approach is too demanding and will cause the dropout rate to soar. But what are the facts? In the last fifteen years, the high school curriculum has been diluted by a tidal wave of new electives. If the proponents of the education-as-entertainment theory are correct, the watering down of the curriculum should have roused student interest and reduced the dropout rate considerably. But that has not happened. Instead, the dropout rate has remained stuck at 25 percent, where it was before the great curriculum revolution of the late sixties. Historically,

✳

the proportion of students who finish high school has changed in response to economic and demographic factors, not the difficulty of the course work.

Critics of traditional education can continue to insist that tougher schools will cause dropout rates to increase, but they haven't a scintilla of evidence to back up their claim. To the contrary, the facts point in just the opposite direction. For instance, an analysis of California testing data shows that among high school sophomores who don't go on to college, those who dropped out scored better as a group on the National Center for Education Statistics's composite test of reading, writing, vocabulary, math, science, and civics than those who stuck it out for their diploma. In other words, students who are smart and enrolled in a general track program get bored, get pregnant, or want a job and leave school. In fact, nearly 20 percent of today's dropouts have I.Q.'s over 120—putting them in the bright to near-genius category. Is the school system too tough for these talented youngsters? Obviously not; if anything, it's not challenging enough. But what about minority students? In a recent national poll, 66 percent of black children (two out of three!) said that school was too easy for them. We are constantly warned that the traditional curriculum is either too difficult or not relevant and will bore street smart black youths to tears. The student polls indicate they're being bored to tears, all right—by an education system whose every move is pitched to an academic lowest common denominator.

When you strip away all the rhetoric, the basic problem with rejecting traditional education as being too difficult for minorities is that it's a racist argument. Racism is an epithet that has been tossed around rather loosely in recent years, but I use it in this context with due deliberation. Racism, according to the dictionary, is the belief that the primary determinant of certain traits and capacities in humans is racial makeup and that, consequently, one race can be judged inherently superior to another. It is racist, by definition, to say that most black or Hispanic children aren't smart enough to cope with an academic course load with which most white children can cope. It is also grossly untrue. And look at the insidious consequences of this patronizing doctrine. Under the guise of compassion (since they can't learn the academic curriculum, we should spare them the misery of trying), this doctrine gives all parties an easy excuse for loafing. Teachers shrug: my students can't do any better, so why should I push them? Many adolescents, not surprisingly, are happy to go along with a cruise down easy street. Make no mistake about it, however; the final destination for this joyride is a dead end. Education uniquely demands, and ultimately rewards, individual effort and hard work. With no experience to confirm that the future can be improved by sacrificing in the present, children can't be expected to understand this equation. Adults must insist on it for them. To the extent that a school system settles for less than maximum effort from each of its students—of whatever color—it isn't doing its job.

The second main argument against the traditional curriculum for minority students is that such a course of studies smacks of cultural imperialism. Particularly in the value-laden humanities, so the argument runs, blacks, Hispanics, native Americans, and Asian-Americans might encounter a world view that is either irrelevant to their own heritage or downright destructive of it. The high-water mark of this viewpoint was reached in the late seventies, when a federal judge ordered Ann Arbor's English teachers to go back to school to learn something called "Black English" so that they could instruct their students in the dialect

✳

of the ghetto. (Does that mean the brilliant oratory of Jesse Jackson isn't "Black English"? What do you suppose James Earl Jones speaks? or Leontyne Price?) The underlying rationale for this bizarre decision was presented in the February 1975 issue of *College English*. Students had a right to "their own patterns and varieties of language—the dialect of their nurture or whatever dialect in which they find their own style," a group of professional educators affirmed. There was no longer any question of "correct" or "incorrect" language. "The claim that any one dialect is unacceptable amounts to an attempt of one social group to exert its dominance over another," their manifesto said.

This is broadmindedness carried to the point of inanity. Education is supposed to open up new vistas for students, not foreclose them. Think of the practical consequences. Just who did the egalitarian professors suppose students of "Black English" were going to dazzle with their superb command of jive—the chairman of the board? An education that prepares children to hang out on neighborhood street corners for the rest of their lives, that isolates them from, rather than ushers them into, the larger worlds of business, science, and government, isn't worthy of the name. This is true for the whole spectrum of "at-risk" kids—inner city, rural, low-income, ethnic, or those from single parent households. As Patricia Albjerg Graham wrote in the Fall 1984 issue of *Daedalus,* to exclude students from the wisdom of our heritage effectively keeps them class-bound and vitiates the potential power of our schools to create opportunity, develop individual talent, and empower students to take part in society.

Unlike teaching in a dialect of English, teaching non-English speaking students in their native tongue (also known as bilingual education) can be a useful program as long as it is kept within reasonable limits. Originally, bilingual education was conceived as a means to ease the transition of non-English speaking students into the regular school program. By the mid-seventies, however, its boosters had begun treating it as an end in itself. In fact, in some areas of California, even English-speaking students of Hispanic descent were being encouraged to pursue their education in Spanish, supposedly as a means of affirming their distinct cultural identity.

The problem with adopting linguistic separatism as an education strategy is obvious. This is an English-speaking country. In my mind, that's not a statement open to debate; it's an overwhelming fact of life. We are a nation of immigrants, or the descendants of immigrants, who hail from every corner of the globe. The Germans, Russians, French, Italians, Poles, and Swedes who came here a century ago didn't much like the idea of learning a new language, but to get ahead economically, they did what they had to. Today the situation is no different. If one wants a shot at the best jobs in the United States—in a profession or business or science—one needs to know English. That's why the contemporary discussion of bilingual education no longer hinges on the political question of whether to mainstream students but rather on the professional question of how best to do it. Quite simply, the function of bilingual education is to teach newcomers enough English so that they can take part in the regular curriculum. The measuring stick of its success is how quickly and effectively it enables students to do so.

Although these ideas about the academic core may sound like plain common sense, some critics brand them as pure reactionary cant. I find it interesting that in the sixties the harshest criticism of the traditional curriculum for minority or working-class students emanated from the political left. Intellectuals such as Michael F. D. Young of England and Pierre Bourdieu of France portrayed the academic disciplines as mere subterfuges for imposing ruling-class values on oppressed groups so that they would cooperate in their own exploitation. Ten years after he published his blockbuster *How Children Fail,* John Holt addressed another question in the March 1982 issue of the *Progressive.* "Can We Save the Public Schools?" asked the title of his article. "No, and They're Not Worth Saving," it answered. Holt went on to describe the public schools as "miniature Fascist states" busy preparing students for a lifetime of slavery.

This blanket condemnation is interesting because it contrasts so vividly with a radical analysis from another, and to my mind, more thoughtful, era. Antonio Gramsci, the Italian Communist jailed by Mussolini, wrote extensively from prison on social matters. He is generally regarded as the foremost Marxist theoretician on education. What did he say, for example, about teaching students in their local dialect? "Someone who only speaks dialect," he wrote, "or understands the standard language incompletely, necessarily has an intuition of the world which is more or less limited and primitive; which is fossilized and mechanistic in relation to the major currents of thought which dominate world history." Gramsci favored teaching the national language as an entrée into the "historic richness and complexity of the great cultures." He also staunchly defended the academic curriculum for all students, the value of hard work, discipline, and high standards in classrooms, and the regular administration of formal tests and examinations. Objective tests are a reflex bugaboo for the contemporary left, but Gramsci favored them and opposed the Fascist attempt to liberalize the Italian examination system by testing such imponderables as creativity and character development. He feared that this "reform" would be used to disguise the intellectual superiority of the gifted but poor child over the less able rich one. When Gramsci attacked the pre-Fascist education system, it wasn't method or curriculum he decried but the limited access of poor students to such desirable training.

You don't have to be a Marxist theoretician to agree with a basic truth that Gramsci was getting at: the common culture belongs to all of us. And every child in this country—rich or poor, male or female, black, brown, red, yellow, or white—is entitled to a crack at it. In the seventies, the political tendency in our society was to fragment into special-interest groups. In education, that tendency translated into the demand that each group have its own tailor-made curriculum on the grounds that the mainstream view was somehow alienating and exclusive. But why should there be an insistence that the common culture belongs only to the elite when, quite clearly, it belongs to everybody? I don't believe there is such a thing as black honesty or Chicano honesty or white honesty. Martin Luther King, Jr. didn't speak just as a black when he harked back to our Biblical and civic traditions in his civil rights speeches. Abraham Lincoln didn't speak just as a white when he talked about what it was going to take for a democracy of the people, by the people, and for the people to endure. Both of these men expressed transcendent ideas that apply to all of us. The wisdom of this country's traditions and heritage is the birthright of every student.

The element of truth in objections to the traditional curriculum as discriminatory is that some subjects, notably history, have been too narrowly framed in the past. The basic ideas were legitimate, but all the exemplars of virtue were stereo-

✳

typically white males. Today's history classes offer a much broader representation of the variety of people who helped shape this country: men and women from every race, creed, and corner of the globe. That's the best solution. If a particular group doesn't like the curriculum, the answer isn't a retreat from the academic disciplines. The answer is to correct the course content. In literature or the arts, local districts should adopt reading lists that recognize the natural desire to maintain an ethnic identity. Quite rightly, black students are entranced by Alex Haley's *Roots* and Richard Wright's *Native Son;* Hispanic students by Jose Villareal's *Pacho* and Peter Matthiessen's *Sal Si Puedes;* Japanese-Americans by Yoshiko Ushida's *Samurai of Gold Hill* and Monica Sone's *Nisei Daughter;* and so on. There are an infinite variety of stories and modes of expression, but they all reinforce the same lofty ideals. My point is that our country was founded on the expectation that out of many traditions one nation could be braided that would be stronger and more durable than any single strand. The public schools are uniquely suited to serve as a forum for discovering the commonalities that bind us together, but only so long as all the constituent elements take part with a will.

It would be nice to report that everyone learned from the dismal results of two decades of lowered expectations and that educators now solidly back a return to standards of excellence as the best hope for disadvantaged youngsters, but it wouldn't be accurate. Chester E. Finn, Jr. in an article for the *American Spectator* outlined the early signs of a backlash against the excellence movement. Not surprisingly, the same hoary arguments about high standards being discriminatory and unfair to minority students are being put forward in defense of the malfunctioning status quo. Iowa education professor James Albrecht says that the new emphasis on academic learning "will only hasten the disenfranchisement of the inarticulate, those whose children are already unsuccessful and demoralized in our schools." And Harvard education professor Charles Willie adds that "elitism has taken over where racism and sexism left off and is performing some of the racist and sexist "dirty work" under the banner of maintaining high standards."

I wish the university professors who author these perfectly well-intentioned but absolutely poisonous sentiments in nominal defense of minority rights had followed me around on my campaign when I spoke with black and Hispanic audiences. A salutary effect of running for and holding a public office is that you hear what the people want. And what minority parents want is a challenging course of studies for their kids. I remember one meeting in particular. Right after my election, Josie Bain, with whom I served on the state school board, arranged a luncheon for me in Los Angeles with the leaders of the black community. The head of the local chapter of the NAACP was there, as were Baptist ministers, business owners, a newspaper editor, a school board member, and several principals. Frankly, I was nervous. Because of the prevailing liberal rhetoric, raising education standards was still perceived as an antiminority position. And the situation wasn't helped by the fact that the incumbent I had just defeated was a black man. I went ahead with my usual pitch in favor of standards and expectations and the need to give kids a sense of ethical connection with the broader society. We have been shortchanging your children, I told the audience, by not expecting enough of them. When I sat down, I braced myself for a volley of skeptical questions, but, to my surprise, the support was overwhelming! "Our kids

✳

are taking a weak program," one speaker after another said. "They don't do enough writing." "They're not being prepared to succeed in college." My criticisms sounded mild in comparison. At last, one principal had the temerity to stand up and say, "What happens if we raise standards? Aren't our kids going to drop out? They'll never make it." I thought the group was going to crucify her on the spot. If a traditional education was good enough for the children of Beverly Hills, that was what they wanted for their kids, too.

Hispanic parents have told me the same thing, as have Hispanic educators with experience on the front lines of the public schools—educators like Pete Mesa, whose "tough love" policies as Superintendent are turning around the Milipitas School District, and Ray Cortines, Superintendent of the San Jose School District. Buying the presence of students at the price of not giving them what they need, these leaders say, is bad for the schools and bad for the kids. All in all, my experience is that the closer you get to the parents of minority children (and the farther away from the comfortably salaried bureaucrats and educational theoreticians who presume to speak on their behalf), the less likely you are to hear complaints that school is too tough. In fact, during all my years at Second Community, I can recall only one instance of such a complaint. We had an in-class library of books—paperbacks picked up at garage sales, mostly—and students were expected to read a certain number of them on their own over the course of each grading period. The parents of a little black girl of ability demanded a conference with the principal. They were upset because I would not allow their daughter to continue choosing her own books the way all the other children did. What they didn't know was my reason for singling her out, which was that she had been selecting books of cartoons—Dennis the Menace, Superman, Peanuts—that were far below her reading level. I told the parents that their daughter would either have to work up to her ability or leave my class. "Isn't that kind of racist?" the mother asked. "No way," I answered. "To let her get away with it would be the most racist thing I could do. Because what I'd be saying is she can't keep up with the white kids, which is absolutely not true."

I tell this story because it illustrates a critical point. Forget the allowance money, nice clothes, and video games. The most important way in which upper-middle-class children are "advantaged" in school is that everyone expects them to perform. Their parents expect them to read on their own. Their teachers expect them to do their homework. Their counselors expect them to sign up for the demanding courses. And by and large, they do all these things—and learn. But no one pushes our inner city youth or, for that matter, the bulk of middle-class children in quite the same way. Instead, what you find too often is what a friend of mine, Gary Sykes, a professor of education at Stanford, calls "The Deal." "The Deal" is an implied contract whose requirements are straightforward but never expressed in so many words. Under the tacit rules of "The Deal," students agree to come to class and not make trouble, and the teacher agrees not to burden them with any expectations more demanding than staying awake. In this way, both students and teacher get what they want with a minimum of effort. The student is awarded a passing grade and eventually a diploma, and the teacher collects his or her salary and eventually retires. The only thing missing in this transaction is the incredible excitement of a bona fide education.

Of course, good students don't want any part of "The Deal," and good teachers and good administrators won't stand for it. It is important to note that there are tens of thousands of hard-working, dedicated teachers keeping the faith in our inner city schools. This is the cadre around which the reform movement is rallying. They need, and deserve, the full support of parents and school administrators in leading the return to lofty academic standards. What they *don't* need is some overwrought faultfinder telling them that the core curriculum they teach is oppressive, that the habit of hard work they encourage is passé, or that their caring enough to insist that minority children get a good start in life somehow qualifies them as racist.

In all candor, however, I predict that resistance to the excellence movement based on the false charge that it is unfair to minority children will increase before this morally sensitive issue is finally put to rest. The awkward truth is that, so far at least, standardized tests have resulted in a higher rate of failure for blacks and Hispanics. For instance, blacks represented 20 percent of Florida's seniors in 1983 but 57 percent of those who failed the high school competency exam. When that state instituted a qualifying test for prospective teachers, 21 percent of white candidates failed, as compared to 65 percent of black ones. Dreadful numbers like these make people suspicious and are bound to have political consequences. Florida's Association of Black Psychologists held a press conference and denounced the tests as "instruments of European cultural imperialism" and urged a black boycott. Nine black students sued for diplomas in spite of having failed the minimum competency test, and a federal judge ruled in their favor. The state of Florida stuck by its guns, however, and in the most recent battery of exams, minority candidates have begun doing much better.

The percentage of minority candidates flunking California's new teacher competency exam has also been disturbingly high (around 74 percent of blacks and 62 percent of Hispanics), but a symptomatic and highly significant reaction has ensued. Black educators have taken the lead in defending the new standards. Bernard Gifford, dean of the University of California's graduate school of education, has publicly rejected the idea that the teacher qualifying test developed by the Princeton-based Educational Testing Service is either racist or useless. He says the test covers basic material every teacher ought to know and goes on to propose a three-step comprehensive program to "interrupt the cycle of failure" among minority candidates. In brief, his proposal calls for early identification of minority and low-income students who have a commitment to teaching; intensive university and postgraduate training for those students, including partial tuition scholarships for high achieving ones; and rewards for those who prove effective once they are in the classroom.

This stand parallels the position of Thomas Arcienega, President of California State University at Bakersfield. When the question of tough admissions standards at the university level arose, Arcienega defended them but also made the point that it can't be just a sink-or-swim proposition. Minority students willing to put forward an honest effort should be helped to make the grade. Sociologist Harry Edwards, a colleague of Bernard Gifford at Berkeley, echoed this idea when he opposed the position of black college presidents and endorsed tougher entrance requirements for college athletes. Writing in the August 1983 issue of *The Atlantic,* Edwards took this hard-nosed stance:

✳

> Outcries of "racism" and calls for black boycotts of
> or exemptions from such tests, seem to me neither
> rational nor constructive long-term responses to the
> problem of black students' low test scores. Culture
> can be learned and taught. Class-specific values and
> perspectives can be learned and taught. And this is
> what we should be about as black educators—pre-
> paring our young people to meet the challenges they
> face on these tests, and, by extension, in this society.

Edwards's reference to black educators is noteworthy. As he
observed in his article, in the sixties black parents from Ocean
Hill–Brownsville in New York to Watts in California complained that white teachers and principals in inner city schools
were indifferent to the progress of their children, and as a result
of these criticisms, changes in staffing were made. Today, many
predominantly black school systems now have a majority of
black teachers and administrators. "Can we afford to be any
less critical when white incompetence is replaced by black incompetence?" Edwards rhetorically demands, and he responds
"Given what is at stake, the answer must be an emphatic and
resounding no. We must let all educators know that if they are
not competent to do their job, they have no business in our
schools."

Reporters have been a little slow catching on to this newly
militant mood. I was on a San Francisco television program
with the head of the local teachers' union and a leading black
educator, Dr. David Bowick, superintendent of Oakland's public
schools. The reporter, who was white, was grilling me about
the high rate of failure among minority applicants on the CBEST

exam. For the sake of providing successful role models to minority kids, he was saying, wouldn't it be better to lower the passing grade for minority teachers? Before I could say a word, Dr. Bowick cut in: "Don't send them to Oakland. Our students are already behind. The last thing they need is a teacher who isn't competent."

We are all working toward the day when standardized exams will result in color-blind outcomes because every test-taker will be equally well prepared. If that means putting more resources into inner city schools, so be it. But the new wave of black and Hispanic reformers are reminding us of something else. While striving to bring about equality of achievement, never again should we become so anxious for the appearance of success that we sacrifice the integrity of the educational process itself—by watering down the core curriculum, lowering standards on the teacher-credentialing exam, or issuing sham diplomas. That way lies disillusionment and disaster.

The one constant in our country's progress over the generations has been the extension of an education to every corner of this democracy. At the turn of the century, 6.3 percent of all youngsters graduated from high school. As recently as 1950, only 59 percent earned diplomas (and only 10 percent of blacks). By 1965, the overall figure had jumped to 75 percent. This influx of new students swamped the system and made it difficult to maintain high academic standards. The history of U.S. education in this century can be viewed as a series of pendulum swings between the progressive urge to hold on to the great mass of students with ever easier, sometimes wholly empty, courses and the essentialist urge to restore the central academic core. The trick, of course, is to accomplish both goals at once: to present the core academic curriculum to the widest number

✳

of students. It can be done. The goals of equality for disadvantaged students and academic excellence are not the irreconcilable horns of a dilemma. Rather, they are two sides of the same coin—the golden sovereign of cultural and scientific literacy for all—which it is the public schools' privilege and responsibility to mint. Minority parents and the gathering school reform movement don't intend to settle for one jot less.

CHAPTER FIVE

From McGuffey's Reader
to Johnny B. Goode

S HORTLY AFTER I took office, I was invited to address
the honors students of the Letters and Sciences College
of the University of California at Los Angeles. In terms
of talent, this group would make absolutely top-notch teachers,
or so I hoped. With all the aplomb of an Army recruiter, I
began rummaging around in my mind for a topic that would
intrigue this highly eligible audience. What would challenge a
group of bright young college students about the new school
reform movement? At last, I hit on a topic as shockingly risqué
by today's standards as it once was absolutely taken for granted:
the proposition that public schools should instruct children on
matters of ethics and morals.

My argument, stripped to the bare bones, went something
like this. Children are not automatically moral or ethical. It
takes a great deal of education, social bolstering, and sustained
effort at putting a culture's highest ideals, values, and inspirations before young people to help them attain their full humanity. That is a difficult task in any society, but doubly so in
the United States because our Enlightenment heritage tends to
emphasize the development of the individual. Schools should

---

enshrine and celebrate the individual, but doing that tends to overshadow the requirements of the community. We should also recognize that our political life demands that we convince students to attach to the group, be it family, church, community, or country. The point is that sheer self-interest has never been a sufficient basis for any society. Our founding fathers pledged their lives, their fortunes, and their sacred honor in defense of shared beliefs—a lofty precedent. Children need to hear about the high ideals of our collective moral order if they are to be lifted out of a self-centered existence. Our democracy and the quality of life depend on enough people making that leap. The alternative is that they will grow up feeling emotionally isolated—strangers to ethics in a devil-take-the-hindmost world. They won't commit to leading moral lives. They will be relegated to a mean and unsatisfying existence. And, inevitably, we will all end up the losers. End of argument.

Apparently, these UCLA honor students had never heard the notion that embracing moral standards could be a liberating experience, not an oppressive one—a disturbing indictment of the quality of their undergraduate education. They were excited by it. We had a lively discussion, I sewed my philosophical seeds, and that would have been that—except for the fact that one of my friends had a daughter in the class. Through her I subsequently learned that at the next class meeting, the professor spent the whole hour trying to undo the havoc I had wrought. He had heard my argument as an extremely reactionary and dangerous one, and posthaste assigned the class a paper on the hazards of the Moral Majority's taking over the schools.

This panicky confusion of my position—that schools should engage students in our ethical tradition—with a whole-hearted embrace of the doctrinaire agenda of Bible-Belt evangelism is, unfortunately, not atypical. The reigning orthodoxy of modern intellectuals, as Daniel Bell has observed, is radical individualism and anything that asserts the interest of the community is bound to strike an uncritical adherent of this position as a threat. Rather than argue the merits of the case, the UCLA professor found it easier to slap on a label—the Superintendent of Public Instruction as the second coming of Jerry Falwell—and make his rebuttal from the presumed moral high ground of defending civil liberties. But I insist on the distinction. There is a difference between those who want group prayer in the public schools (the practice of religion) and those who want moral content in the curriculum (a fundamental purpose of the schools, as we have already defined it). Between the equally unacceptable poles of religious dogmatism and institutionalized public amorality, there is room for a rational discussion of what ideals and standards we as a society hold to be worthy of praise and emulation. Bob Bellah in his recent book *Habits of the Heart* advocates a tempered individualism, emphasizing both individual freedom and community commitment. The fact that many educators fail to discern this middle ground is one index of our current predicament.

Let's take a closer look at the issue. The belief that a public school is no place to teach values rests on a pair of misconceptions. The first is that morality and ethics smack of the religious and spiritual and that teaching them in a public school necessarily violates the constitutionally guaranteed separation of church and state. The second objection is more pragmatic: it holds that, in a pluralistic society such as our own, agreement on what moral values should be conveyed could never be reached. It follows from this premise that such an attempt could only be construed as an illegitimate use of Big Brother's coercive power.

This is nonsense. The constitutional argument is plainly wrong. The First Amendment reads: "Congress shall make no law respecting an establishment of religion, or prohibiting the free exercise thereof." It does *not* say: "Congress shall be aggressively neutral on matters of ethics, morals, and virtue, and any discussion of shared values in the public sector is strictly prohibited." To the contrary, with their unselfconscious references to "Nature's God," "the Creator," and "divine Providence" in the Declaration of Independence (and throughout the nation's seminal documents), it is clear that the founding fathers were themselves spiritual men. They were not against the practice of religion in general and certainly not against the transmission of elevated moral sentiments in schools. What they sought to prohibit was the establishment of a single state religion in the European mold. This prohibition poses no difficulty, however, because there is no question of teaching a particular creed— Catholic, Baptist, Jewish, Mormon, Buddhist, or whatever— in the public schools. The question is whether or not our schools will again undertake to reinforce at the level of general social consensus the moral and ethical lessons that the child is learning at home.

I say the schools should do so. The vigilant civil libertarians who bring up objection number two say they should not, because the social consensus of which I speak does not exist. But they are wrong about their vision of "America the Contrary": 58 percent of the population attend church or temple on a regular basis, a far higher proportion than in any other developed country. And 95 percent of U.S. citizens say they believe in God. Schools shouldn't be run by majority vote, but they are an expression of the public will, and when it comes to moral instruction, the numbers are overwhelming. In September of

1984, the Gallup Poll released its annual survey of U.S. attitudes toward education. For the survey, the public had been asked to rate the relative importance of various goals for the public schools on a scale of zero to ten. The alternatives included everything from preparing students for a high-paying job to training them to take part in our democracy, to promoting physical fitness, to showing students how to use a computer. The results? Out of twenty-five possibilities listed, the second-highest show of approval was accorded the following goal: "To develop standards of what is right and wrong." Indeed, the only educational goal that outscored moral formation (and just barely) was this classic academic mission: "To develop the ability to speak and write correctly." Clearly, the expectation among the people in this country is that education should include some kind of moral and ethical training. But what kind? In order to answer that question, I would like to turn our attention first to a perfect example of how *not* to do it—by means of a program known as "values clarification."

Along with so many other revolutionary bromides, the values clarification movement made its intellectual debut on the public school stage at the beginning of the seventies. Its chief spokesman, Sidney Simon of the University of Massachusetts School of Education, explained the rationale for the new approach. The old "moralizing" method of passing on to students the values of the community—a suspicious practice also referred to as inculcation, imposition, indoctrination, or brainwashing—was no longer acceptable. It wasn't acceptable because enlightened types like Simon had come to a radical *aperçu*, namely, that "none of us has the 'right' set of values to pass on to other people's children." Instead of brainwashing students, Simon advised, the modern teacher—that is, "values processor"—should help them identify "their own feelings, their own ideas, their own beliefs, so that the choices and decisions they make are deliberate, based on their own value system." Values clarification, relying on questionnaires called "strategies," was presented as the way to accomplish this liberating goal. The technique was a miracle of flexibility. By filling out the appropriate "strategies," students could find out how they really felt about such diverse matters as how they spent their leisure time, hit-and-run drivers, the seasons of the year, and euthanasia.

The appeal of this approach was evident. It kept the educators in the business of talking about what the public wanted them to talk about—issues of right and wrong—but it removed the nasty onus of imposing authoritarian judgments on innocent youth (or, for that matter, of taking any position at all on questions of deep value). Judgment became the exclusive preserve of the students. Teachers were allowed in the classroom as "facilitators" whose job was to keep the conversation rolling. Values clarification proved immensely popular. Handbooks on it were written for everything from home economics classes to Girl Scout troups. By 1975, thousands of school programs relied on it, and ten states had adopted it as the official model for their moral education programs.

Unfortunately, there's something absolutely essential missing from values clarification, and that's values, as the word is generally understood. While pretending to Olympian detachment in its neutrality on moral issues, values clarification actually affirms the shallowest kind of ethical relativism. It tells students that on matters of profound moral significance, their opinion—no matter how ill-informed, far-fetched, or speciously reasoned—is all that counts. Ethics and morals are reduced to matters of personal taste. The issues of abortion and

＊

registering for the draft are weighed on the same personal, idiosyncratic scale as one's choice of spring clothing or vacation destination: it is so if you say it's so.

This blithe invitation to moral anarchy, however, is not the way the world works. Our society is built on widely observed moral precepts. It isn't a matter of personal conjecture, for example, whether stealing a Walkman from a classmate's locker is right or wrong. It's wrong, and so is cheating. However, students who decide that they personally sanction using crib notes because tests are irrelevant to the real dynamic of learning, or because the teacher assigned too much material to study in so little time, or for any one of a thousand convenient reasons, are perfectly entitled to do so under the values clarification rubric. Conceding the point, a teacher put it this way: "Once you accept the idea that kids have the right to build a position with logical arguments, you have to accept what they come up with."

This is arrant nonsense, of course, but values clarification sanctions such sophisms. It uses the Socratic method of question and answer but forgets about Socrates' passionate search for a truth that is accessible to all. Worst of all, values clarification is a self-conscious abdication of the adult role in education. It says to children that we adults don't hold anything sacred, that we don't believe in anything deeply enough to stand up for it, that the cumulative wisdom of our collective culture over 3000 years of struggle and progress can be reduced to two magic words: suit yourself.

If students were born with the discerning integrity of Mahatma Gandhi, the concern for others of Albert Schweitzer, the harmonious self-discipline of Confucius, and the seasoned judgment of King Solomon, values clarification would be a fine pedagogical tool. But everything we know from the litrature of the developmental psychology of childhood and adolescence suggests that moral character is painstakingly acquired, not pulled out of a hat, but earned in predictably sequenced stages, over time. In fact, following the lead of Jean Piaget in the study of cognitive development, contemporary researchers such as Lawrence Kohlberg and Jane Loevenger have identified a pattern of development that characterizes moral growth in children and transcends cultural boundaries. Very briefly, it goes something like this: Beginning with an infantile awe in the presence of a magically potent adult world, the child first learns to behave out of a desire for reward or fear of punishment (commonly, the fear of withdrawal of parental affection). An important leap occurs when the youngster adopts the conventional mores of his or her family or school chums, out of a wish to fit in, or later, out of a sense of loyalty to the group and emotional identification with it. Eventually, the young adult breaks away, appraises the moral principles that have governed his or her life, and consciously chooses to accept some of them on rational grounds. As the individual matures, his or her ethical perspective will continue to broaden.

This scheme can be embroidered at considerable length and there is some dispute about the details, but I think most parents will recognize the general progression from dependence to independence and from self-concern, through conformity, to conscious election of the good. The conclusion to be drawn from all these findings is plain: the adult world has a critical responsibility to discharge. It must furnish the child with a guiding morality in the form of expectations and good habits. With this foundation, the young adult can either adopt that guiding morality later on or formulate one of his or her own.

✳

The problem with values clarification is that it short-circuits the process of growing up. It asks children to make moral choices at a time when most of them are not prepared, by experience or in emotional terms, to do so. As psychologist Bruno Bettelheim put it, "The mistake today is that too many believe what ripe maturity can contain is the best fare for immaturity."

We have to keep reminding ourselves that it isn't patronizing to treat children like children—it's parental. At the heart of moral education is a paradox. Nineteenth-century sociologist Émile Durkheim expressed it best when he said, "Solely by imposing limits can a child be liberated." We want free citizens who, as an assertion of their humanity and moral identity, consciously decide to expend the enormous ethical effort it takes to be another Gandhi, Schweitzer, or Confucius. But to reach this ethical peak, we must be willing to approach the problem like a good mountaineering team. We must provision the base camps that make possible the final attempt. If the goal is a refined morality in adults, the starting point is instilling a clear sense of right and wrong in children.

The home is the primary locus of moral formation, of course, and religious instruction can be a key element. But the schools must participate, too, along with the other social institutions. A traditional education orients the students to the high ethical expectations of the community both by what it teaches and by how it goes about it. In the traditional setting, students learn the value of self-discipline when they turn in homework assignments, of courtesy when they raise a hand before answering, of punctuality when they come to class on time. The teacher, as an exemplar of the adult world, is a closely scrutinized role model. Does he or she prepare well for class every day, and grade fairly? Is he or she good-humored, inspirational, compassionate, honest, and respectful of differences? No one could measure up to such an impossible standard of perfection, but the best teachers try.

The other hugely important source of moral insight for the student in the traditional scheme is the course content itself, particularly in the humanities. Exposure to the cultural heritage carries with it a powerful message. Think of the great stories in our tradition: Icarus flying toward the sun on wings of wax, Oliver Twist asking for a second bowl of gruel, Nathan Hale dying for his country, Penelope remaining faithful despite the long absence of her husband. These stories speak to us with great force about the perils of pride and greed and the honor of patriotism and fidelity. In the end, the moral sensibility and social conscience of a civilization can only be learned by reading and discussing the classic works of its literature and history and the biographies of its exemplars.

We have always known this truth. Just look at the texts used to teach children in the nineteenth century, when people naturally assumed that the primary business of school was to train character. *McGuffey's Reader,* used in the first through sixth form, was the most famous of these texts, but they all resemble one another. In their pages, God was everywhere and operated according to a stern system of dire punishments and bankable rewards. The disobedient boy was drowned; the honest waif who declined to steal a gold watch was adopted by its owner. Patriotic biographies of George Washington and Benjamin Franklin appeared with pointed allegories about Mr. Idle and Mr. Toil. I'm not recommending a return to *McGuffey's Reader* for today's public schools. Its insistent morality was that of an agrarian nation, prizing Victorian ideals that were retributive and harsh. Its Horatio Alger themes would be entirely too narrow to instruct the children of a much more cosmopolitan and diverse society. Still, these texts were on to something—the power of stories to edify as they entertain. Our challenge is to identify their modern equivalent, to put before students the lives and legends and stories and speeches that adequately express the guiding morality of our modern, democratic, pluralistic society.

I say "guiding" for two reasons: first, because the distillation of adult wisdom the schools present is only a starting point, but a crucial one, in the adolescent's quest for a personal identity and value system; and second, because the best expression of this morality (as opposed to what Walter Lippmann called the "eternal verities" at the heart of it) is changing over time, which is the cause of the dated quality of the old readers. Still, I don't think there needs to be a lot of hand-wringing over identifying a new set of common values. The Japanese samurai had their code of Bushido; citizens of Athens revered the standard of *kalos kagathos,* or versatility, grace, and spirit; the medieval church warned against the seven deadly sins of pride, anger, sloth, envy, greed, gluttony, and lust and upheld their virtuous antitheses. Every civilization has a distinctive set of moral and ethical imperatives it seeks to pass on to its children, and ours is no exception.

What might that guiding morality look like? No doubt the key concepts would include such broad principles as the sanctity of human life, respect for the dignity of the individual, and the importance of the family and personal moral effort. The guarantees flowing out of the principle of the individual's primacy—the guarantees of freedom of speech, religion, association, and the press, of equality before the law, of respect for property rights and the system of free enterprise—have been encoded in the law of the land. But, to make a good man or woman, our republican and Biblical traditions tell us, more is required. Thus, the vast majority of us would agree that a good person is generous to others, not miserly or self-absorbed; modestly self-assured, not vain or boastful; faithful, not promiscuous; prudent, not rash or prodigal; reverent to the elderly, not brusque or insolent; optimistic, not envious; forgiving, not vengeful; hospitable, discrete, loving, patient, not hostile, overbearing, cold, or slapdash. The list goes on—but you get the idea. It just isn't that difficult to arrive at a consensus about what our society admires.

At Hunter's Point, we had as diverse a group of parents in terms of ethnic background, income, and lifestyle as you could imagine. Our parents were very active in every aspect of running the school, including helping out in classes. But we had no arguments about moral content. Why not? I think the best explanation is that parents trust the implicit wisdom of the collective past. They understand that steeping the students in the ideas, personalities, and stories of our civilization is not an indoctrination that warps but rather one that does the opposite. What could be more liberating and offer a greater diversity than that tradition?

Our literature is hardly monolithic. Take a central concept like the rule of law. A student might read *The Ox Bow Incident* by Willem von Tilberg Clark. In it, some angry ranchers catch a group of what they take to be cattle rustlers, and after finding some pretty damning circumstantial evidence, string 'em up, despite their pleas of innocence. But it turns out the "rustlers" really *are* innocent. The novel is an emotionally taut explication of why we shouldn't tolerate vigilantes in our society. Soon enough, however, the same student is going to run into *Bleak House* by Charles Dickens. This time, the plot revolves around a lawsuit over a will. Through the course of the book, the case of *Jarndyce* v. *Jarndyce* drags on in the Court of Chancery, supporting dusty legions of clerks and solicitors. It concludes when the costs have absorbed the full sum of the fortunes involved. While not the sole theme of the novel, this caution about the suffocating perils of litigiousness shows the reader the dangers of too much law and order even as *The Ox Bow Incident* shows the dangers of too little.

Our literature has a way of deflating ideologues and true believers of every stripe. Are you a laissez-faire capitalist? Then read Frank Norris's *The Octopus,* and squirm. An unregenerate Bolshevik? Try Arthur Koestler's *Darkness at Noon.* Pacifists should be sure to read *The Diary of Anne Frank* or William Shakespeare's *Henry V.* And Marine Corps recruits should study Stephen Crane's *The Red Badge of Courage* or Erich Remarque's *All Quiet on the Western Front.* The wonderful thing about these books isn't that they neutralize each other like some literary version of television's equal-time rule. They make their claim to the truth clearly, passionately, and unequivocally. And in the purifying fire of their complex visions, they refine the moral character of the reader.

Biography works the same way. Teachers complain that today's youth are apathetic. The world is too large and complex and fouled-up, they say, for any individual to make a difference. Students seem to have lost the capacity for moral indignation or outrage. Robert M. Hunt, a professor of government at Harvard, teaches a course on the Holocaust. Recently, he reports, the majority of his students have taken the view that the rise of Hitler and the Nazis was inevitable, that no one could have stopped it, and that in the end, no one was responsible for the slaughter of six million Jews. Hunt calls this blasé view of the past "no-fault history." But there's a forceful corrective to such inanition of the spirit: show students examples of individuals who *did* make a difference. No one could prevent the Holocaust? Let them study the life of Raoul Wallenberg, the daring Swedish diplomat who is credited with singlehandedly saving 100,000 Jews in Budapest. The world is too large, complex, and fouled up? It wasn't too large for Charles Lindbergh in the *Spirit of St. Louis* to risk his life making the first trans-Atlantic flight, or too complex for Watson and Crick to crack the riddle of the double helix, or too fouled up for Mother Teresa, a woman of spirit and quiet determination, to make a significant difference in the back streets of Calcutta. There are heroes among us. Students need the example of such lives as inspirations for their own.

Edmund Burke observed, "The lines of morality are not like the ideal lines of mathematics." Teaching students about our core beliefs will never be like conducting a class in algebra. There will always be differences of opinion, particularly as the discussion becomes more advanced and subtle. But that doesn't mean such instruction can't be done. The best approach is to stick to areas of broad public consensus, especially in the early grades when that indispensable conviction about right and wrong is being formed. We know, for instance, that when people in this country are asked what is most important to them, 4 percent say "making a lot of money," 7 percent say "a fulfilling career," 13 percent say "developing as an individual," and 77 percent say "my family life"; also, 86 percent believe that extramarital sex is wrong. That's a pretty strong argument for treating sexual responsibility as a consensual value.

Conversely, nothing can damage the credibility of the public school as a forum for moral development faster than politicizing it. The classroom is not the place for settling adult squabbles. Both the left and the right have been guilty of this trespass recently. For instance, children should not be taught that all those who oppose the nuclear freeze are warmongers, nor that all those who favor a woman's right to an abortion are murderers. A public consensus (not to be confused with a majority in the opinion polls) does not exist on these issues. When controversial subjects come up (and they should not come up in elementary school), teachers can provide information, make clear the serious nature of the issues, and emphasize that students should reach their decisions on logically defensible and ethically consistent grounds. Students should consult their parents. And they should consult their consciences. But, in contrast to an ethical discussion of a situation involving clear right and wrong, teachers should not put forward their opinion as authoritative.

When it comes to developing good character in students, I don't think that organized prayer in the public schools is the answer. A student is already free to pray at any time, in school or out, as an individual. But when a time is set aside for group devotion and the expectation is created that all students should join in, then I think a legitimate question arises about the separation of church and state. Besides, by the time a government committee got through writing a prayer that everyone could agree on, the net result would be so nebulous as to lose the point of the exercise. This country's ethos is that we respect the rights of minorities and in this case that means that the majority of children will continue to do their community praying where they always have—in churches and synagogues and other meeting places.

At its best, our humanistic tradition does uplift and inspire. My final rebuttal to those who resist a policy of moral education in the public schools is, simply, that they consider the alternative. If we refuse our children the guidance they need in negotiating the passage to adulthood, they will look for group values elsewhere, in the sentimental and violent world of television or in the tumultuous and ethically confused world of their peers. Nature abhors a vacuum; and as the adult world's confidence in its message recedes, the peer group will naturally come forward to fill the void. A chilling example from California comes to mind. In the fall of 1981 in the blue-collar community of Milpitas, a high school student on drugs raped and murdered his girl friend and disposed of the body on a hill outside town. In separate visits, the boy took several of his classmates to the scene of the crime. Word spread through the school and groups began to make the trip out to see the body on their own. It wasn't until two days later that one of the students told a parent and the police were tipped.

Admittedly, this incident is an extreme case of adolescent alienation from the ethical norms of the adult world. But, when you look at the sociological indicators, it's apparent that, as our institutions have put on the mask of official amorality over the last twenty years, the signs of social pathology in our young have soared. Since the mid-sixties, the suicide rate among teenagers has tripled, and the incidence of drug use and alcoholism has climbed substantially, as has the number of teenage pregnancies. Campus psychologists say that an inability to form relationships has become the single greatest problem of today's youth.

Obviously, educators do not bear sole responsibility for these symptoms of social anomie. But they do bear some. In retrospect, it's apparent that the public schools took the easy way out in the late sixties. A serious discussion of deep values can be controversial in a pluralistic society so we found a way to avoid it—by feigning moral neutrality. But that's an illusory victory. It's not good for our children and it's not what the people want. The people do want the schools to be intellectually objective, but they also want them to convey a challenging moral and ethical message. Students need the best wisdom of our civilization before them, constantly pushing them to be the best they can be, to set high ethical standards, and to examine their lives. Growing up isn't easy. The child is born with a yearning for humanity but needs help from the adult world to attain it. The public schools can provide that help. Indeed, that may be their unique and essential purpose in the United States—to bind together a diverse and pluralistic society by disseminating the guiding morality that inheres in our best literature and history. The education reform movement is aiming to make that happen, so that all our children once again may encounter the full meaning of their humanity.

CHAPTER SIX

The California Experience

THE TRADITIONAL education program described
thus far is not just an idealist's pipe dream. I believe
it is the only reform program with a fighting chance
to save the public schools, because it is the only one that all the
key constituencies will support. And you can't get more pragmatic than that. In this chapter, we look at a case history of
school reform, examining how and why the traditional education agenda has prevailed in the rough-and-tumble world of
California politics.

In 1982, on the morning after my rags-to-riches campaign
climaxed with an improbable 800,000-vote victory that put me
in the driver's seat of the nation's largest public school system,
the euphoria rapidly ebbed and a sense of the enormity of the
task ahead settled in. The basic problem was as obvious as it
was intractable: California's public schools were not performing. By every yardstick available—results on standardized exams, the dropout rate, enrollment in academic courses—the
schools had been in decline since the late sixties. There were
bright spots here and there, to which we pointed during the
campaign, schools like El Camino High School in Sacramento

and Menlo Park Elementary, or districts like Huntington Beach or Modesto City Unified. But these successful paradigms of traditional education in practice were few and far between, and there were formidable obstacles in the way of turning the situation around.

The first handicap was widespread public skepticism about the possibility of improvement. According to the Field Poll, 61 percent of Californians thought that the public school system in their community was worse than it used to be. But the majority also doubted whether spending more money would improve the quality of education. This lack of confidence hurt because, in point of fact, the schools were in dire financial straits. Following the Proposition 13 property-tax revolt in 1978, funding for public schools had shifted dramatically from the local districts to the state treasury. But state finances hadn't kept pace with rapid inflation. For example, while California once ranked sixth in the country in terms of the proportion of personal income devoted to public schools, by 1980 it was close to last—number forty-eight out of fifty. Many teachers had been forced to accept cuts in their real income of 15 to 20 percent over the span of five years. According to the Stanford Path Study, one of the reasons that the amount of homework assigned had declined was that many districts simply didn't have enough textbooks for students to take home. The San Jose School District, the eighth largest in California, shut down one-sixth of its schools, cut out one of six periods from its school day, and laid off one-fourth of its teachers, one-third of its administrators, and all of its guidance counselors; and it was still forced to declare bankruptcy when it couldn't meet its bills.

Even with such a backdrop of crisis, however, the political prospects for more school funding in 1982 didn't look good.

✳

In the race for governor, Republican State Senator George Deukmejian had edged out the Democratic mayor of Los Angeles, Tom Bradley, on the strength of the absentee ballot count and a categorical promise not to raise taxes. But, in the midst of a recession, the state treasury was already bare. And, with no new taxes, it wasn't clear where the money to bail out the schools would come from.

In terms of the reform agenda itself, the state's educators were anything but united behind the themes I had enunciated in my campaign. The most influential legislative lobbying group, the teachers' unions, had supported my opponent with large contributions and endorsements and so had the majority of school administrators. On the day after my election, a number of teachers came to school wearing black armbands.

At about this time, I remember speaking to the Sacramento Press Club concerning my master plan for education reform. It was a luncheon, and, as it turned out, I was the main course. The press can be brutally frank. After my speech, their basic line of questioning followed a relentless logic: my ideas about school funding collided head-on with the governor's budget and he had a veto; my reform ideas were unloved by the education lobbying groups and they had the ear of the Democratically controlled assembly and senate. What made me think that my grand plans had the proverbial snowball's chance in hell?

Obviously, I wasn't going to accomplish anything by myself. To rededicate the schools to excellence there needed to be consummate teamwork and cooperation reaching all the way to the classroom level, or it wouldn't happen at all. Nevertheless, I thought I saw a real opportunity for success. (And as it turned out, I was seeing more clearly than the purveyors of conventional wisdom.) By 1982, the political reality in California was that the school debate had reached an impasse. One side, the liberals, had gotten used to arguing the case of the teachers' union. The only thing wrong with the schools, they said, was that they were scandalously underfunded. Give the schools more money and they would do the job. But with a few notable exceptions, the people on this side could not be convinced to take on the issue of quality or reform. The people on the other side, a segment of the Republican caucus and the governor's office, were saying, "Get rid of collective bargaining, teacher tenure, and the rest of the rules that build in mediocrity." They would cheerfully talk all day about issues of quality in education. But they argued, as for money, the schools already had plenty of it if they just spent it more efficiently.

The secret of breaking this impasse was to establish a linkage, to offer educators and legislators a *quid pro quo*: more school money in exchange for quality reform. But this wasn't a message the legislature or the governor was going to accept coming from me. They had to hear it from their constituents, in massive numbers. To get a reform and funding bill into law, what we were really facing was a second campaign, this time to stir up the biggest political ground swell in California since that supporting Proposition 13.

First, though, we had to do the family linen—convince the professional educators to sign on. To form a working group, I reached out to the School Boards Association and to some key administrators. They quickly saw the logic of the trade-off. My proposed carrot was a $950-million increase in education funding, about three times what the governor had budgeted. Even at that figure, California would be spending $200 less per pupil than the average state in the United States.

✳

But the increase would be enough to get educators to stop worrying about survival and to turn their attention back to excellence. In exchange, school leaders were willing to commit to attaining quality at the local level through more homework, better discipline, and higher expectations; to support statewide graduation standards and provisions that would make it easier to fire incompetent teachers and expel troublemakers; and to agree to a whole list of other reforms. Their quick acquiescence was a pleasant surprise and reminded me of an incident during the campaign. I had given a speech to a group of school superintendents in Sonoma County. At the end, one of them stood up and challenged me, saying, "My community doesn't want its kids to take more math, science, and English. And parents will complain if we increase the homework load." "Well," I answered, "the rest of the people in California want those things." And he replied, "If you win, I'll support you. But if you lose, I'll stick to what I've been doing." No doubt, the one-sided results of the election campaign made my early missionary work among school leaders a lot easier.

With the school leadership starting to rally around the flag, the next step was to put together the key elements of a coalition for excellence. The demography of California is very interesting. Right now, about 25 percent of our students are Hispanic, about 10 percent are black, and 6 or 7 percent are Asian; by 1990, it's going to be half minority and half white, and a third of all students in the system will be Hispanic. Obviously, wholehearted support from minority groups is essential for any school program to be legitimate. From the campaign, we already had good backing among Hispanic groups who were dissatisfied with the quality of education their children had been receiving. Because my opponent in the election was black, I expected a little more fence mending would be required with the black community. But, when we made the pitch for excellence and high expectations to black leaders in Oakland, Los Angeles, and San Francisco, the response was enthusiastic; the audiences themselves suggested that the main victims in the decline of the public school standards had been their children. So the minority community committed to the reform package early on. In fact, the chief sponsor of the final bill in the state assembly, Teresa Hughes (Democrat, Los Angeles), is a black legislator. And in the senate, we were lucky enough to have Senator Gary Hart (Democrat, Santa Barbara), a longtime education activist and reform leader, shepherding the bill.

That left the business community. During the campaign, my strongest backing in business circles had come from Silicon Valley. "Our raw material is brain power," David Bossen, the president of Measurex, had answered when a reporter asked him why he endorsed me. "The declining test scores make us concerned that we are running out of a precious resource. We're not graduating enough engineers and scientists to support our continued growth." Building on that base, I began speaking to business groups all over the state, such as the Kiwanis, Rotary, and local chambers of commerce. The people in these groups asked good, skeptical questions. After I addressed the San Diego Chamber of Commerce, for instance, one of its members responded to what I had said this way: "If one of my employees came in and admitted he hadn't been doing the job but said he wanted a raise anyway, I'd toss him out on his ear. Why should we treat you any differently?" And I answered, "That's right. But what would you do if one of your divisions had been posting a loss, and the manager came in and told you, 'Here's my plan to correct the problem. But it's going to take some

money to make the necessary changes'?" The business community saw that logic as valid and jumped on board.

By March of 1983, we had built some real momentum. We
announced our comprehensive reform package at a press conference in Sacramento. The whole coalition—minority leadership, business leadership, and school leadership (although the
teachers' unions were still hanging back)—was there, standing
up and saying, "We're for quality education." It looked like
the legislature was starting to tilt our way and, significantly,
that a core of the Republican leadership was willing to go to
bat for the public schools. At this point, however, Governor
Deukmejian decided to discipline the troops. In a speech before
the Association of California School Administrators, he made
clear his support for public education but reiterated his stand
that school funding would not come at the expense of ruining
his state budget. "Somebody has to play Scrooge," he said. I
spoke after him and in my response reminded the discouraged
administrators, "You have to remember how that story turns
out."

The struggle was coming down to a test of loyalties. The
governor had a legitimate claim on the allegiance of the Republican lawmakers, who could sustain his line-item veto of
the school funding package if they voted as a block. On the
other hand, the voters whom the legislators represented had an
even greater claim—and the means to enforce it. We literally
redoubled our grass-roots organizing efforts.

My wife Nancy took over this operation. For years, Nancy
had tolerated my involvement in education as a kind of eccen-
tric obsession. She realized that I was never going to make
enough money as a teacher to support our family of four children, so she went out and started her own business setting up

financial systems for medical facilities. Soon she had widened the scope of her company and built it into a huge success—so much so that "Sixty Minutes" asked us in 1981 to appear on a segment about couples in which the wife makes vastly more money than the husband. Nancy tells a story (which I take with a grain of salt) about an incident during the taping of that show that started to change her mind about the importance of education. Before the cameras were set up, Harry Reasoner was joking with our children and asked them, "Who do you respect more: your mother, who has gone out and done all these great things, or your dad, who's a teacher?" "I was all full of puff," Nancy says, "I knew the kids were going to say me, because they used to joke about going to work for my company after they graduated from college. But they didn't. They said their dad, because he really believed in something." If Nancy was converted to the cause late in the day, she has been like St. Paul ever since. She sold her business to help finance my run for office and devoted herself full-time for the last three years to organizing, speaking, and cajoling on behalf of the excellence agenda. In our campaign to convince the legislature, she was the schools' secret weapon.

Here's how we went about it. During the election we had met a lot of people from local civic and parents groups who had organized to support their schools. Relying on these contacts and setting up comparable committees in those areas of the state without a ready-made source of help, we went to work. Each committee was furnished with a step-by-step blueprint explaining our legislative goals and recommending tactics such as letter writing, news releases, editorials, participation in phone-in radio shows, breakfast meetings, delegation visits, huge rallies—anything to get the message across to Sacramento that the public cared about this issue. The Bakersfield-based Kern County Alliance for Quality Schools was a paradigm of how effective these committees could be. It ended up with sixty-five people on its advisory board, including the mayor, the head of the local newspaper, and representatives from the petroleum industry and the insurance, banking, and legal professions. David Cartnal, a prominent local architect, was the chairperson. A computer printout showing the key financial supporters of Kern County's assembly members and senators was provided to Cartnal, and he, in turn, served as matchmaker, assigning an influential local friend of education to lobby a lawmaker on behalf of the public schools.

Some unheard of things started to happen. A self-organized group in Orange County held a rally for public schools, and on a Friday evening, 9000 people showed up, enough to fill a football stadium. Over 500,000 letters and postcards poured into Sacramento. The whole campaign seemed to enjoy a wonderful bipartisan immunity. For instance, on May 3, I started out the day as the guest of noted Hollywood liberal Sheldon Andelson at a breakfast at the stylish restaurant Trumps. The audience I addressed included such Democratic luminaries as Stanley Sheinbaum, Yvonne Burke, and former governor Jerry Brown. When those festivities concluded, we drove down the freeway directly to the heart of conservative power, the boardroom of the Fluor Corporation in Irvine, where Bob Fluor hosted a lunch attended by forty of the top executives in the area. I gave exactly the same speech in both places. If there's one institution that everyone is ready to support in this society, it's the public schools.

By this time, the heat was on in Sacramento and versions of the reform legislation had passed both the assembly and the senate by wide margins. In the course of a statewide radio address, Governor Deukmejian raised his bid on the education sweepstakes by $100 million—to $450 million—which was still less than half the increase I thought the schools needed and what it would take to get the teacher groups to accept the reforms. The governor had a legitimate argument to make—the state was so strapped for money it had been forced to issue IOUs to its employees to cover the last few days of the fiscal year. But the schools were on the wrong end of a five-year fiscal slide, and I just didn't think that the public would rather see them continue to deteriorate than, say, raise taxes on alcohol and cigarettes. Politically, we had a once-in-a-lifetime opportunity to usher in the needed reforms; it might not be possible in the next legislative session. The question was, who could convince the governor of that? I had a clipping from the *Los Angeles Times* listing the chief executive officers of California's 100 biggest corporations. I started calling them up. Stuart Buchalter of Standard Brands Paint turned out to be an old classmate at Boalt. But most of the conversations began cold turkey, with me explaining the situation and asking for help. Specifically, what I wanted was a letter sent to the governor saying that the public schools deserved full funding, even if that meant raising taxes. Forty-seven of the chief executive officers I contacted did indeed send such letters, including Roy Anderson of Lockheed, Bob Fluor of Fluor Corporation, Cornell Maier of Kaiser Aluminum, Peter Magowan of Safeway, Carl Reichardt of Wells Fargo Bank, John Young of Hewlett Packard, James Harvey of Transamerica, and Phil Schlein of Macy's.

The great California education debate reached its crisis on June 30, the day on which the state budget was supposed to be decided by law and the eve of a Fourth of July holiday visit by

✳

President Reagan as well. The President's Commission had recently issued its "Excellence in Education" report, and the President was scheduled to attend a conference at Pioneer High School near Los Angeles to showcase his concern. I was there, of course, and absolutely thrilled that we had a President who was willing to lend the prestige of his office to the reform agenda. On the question of finances, however, things were a little more bumpy. Pioneer High School is an academic success story in a poor, largely Hispanic neighborhood. While making the rounds of the classrooms, President Reagan stopped to chat, and a student told him that next year the school might have to cut back to a five-period day because of lack of funds. (Under the Deukmejian budget, the district would have lost 15 percent of its teachers.) "What do you think of that?" the student asked. "Well, I wasn't aware of that," Reagan answered. But times were tough in California, he reasoned, "so everyone may have to be set back a little bit." That was the story that made the *Los Angeles Times* the next morning. It was probably sheer coincidence, but on the evening of the President's visit, I got a phone call from the governor's office offering to double the school budget increase.

When all the dust finally settled, the schools ended up with $850 million of the $950 million I had originally requested along with a package of sixty-five separate reforms, including mandated graduation requirements for all students, a longer school day and year, money for textbooks and summer school, a crack down on discipline and dismissal procedures, an achievement test for seniors to receive honors at graduation, a program of college-loan assumption for new teachers in science and math, and so on. One of the most innovative reforms was a new "mentor teacher" concept. Under its provisions, outstanding teachers can split their time between conducting their own classes and giving tips to new teachers or developing curriculum. They receive a stipend of $4000. The program keeps excellent teachers in the classroom but gives them the possibility of a career stepping-stone. In addition, since it operates on the principle of extra pay for extra work, it skirts the union objection to a master teacher program, that is, that it's unfair to the rest of the teachers.

In all candor, however, the reforms passed in the omnibus California school bill of 1983 were largely symbolic. They were good, sound, structural changes, but the real battle for quality education is in the classroom and school. 1983 was a watershed year in the reform movement because it put educators on notice. It showed that the public was willing, that it even demanded, to pay for the legitimate needs of the school system. But it wouldn't support business as usual. The terms of the promissory note were money for improvement. Since 1983, Governor Deukmejian had made education his "number one priority" and he and the legislature have advanced almost three and one-half billion additional dollars in the name of educational excellence. But to hold this support educators clearly have to deliver.

Although there is renewed public confidence in their integrity and dedication, it's going to take five to ten years for the reforms to jell and make a difference in student performance. I think the public will give us the time we need if we demonstrate our sincerity. And the best way to do that is by setting targets and agreeing to be measured by the results. In California, we have implemented such an accountability program, the first of its kind in the nation. In some ways, the accountability program is an artifact of the computer age and of our exponentially greater ability to manipulate relevant data on school performance these days. At its best, it's a powerful new tool for both educators and the public to use in keeping track of school effectiveness and as a spur to progress.

The first phase of our accountability program was deciding what indices of school health should be used as statewide targets. In April of 1983, the California Department of Education issued a discussion paper that was circulated to the school districts and served as the basis for regional meetings in every county in the state. In this paper, we proposed eight statewide targets, which had been carefully selected in order to measure the progress of children at every level of ability. For instance, for below-level students, we looked at the dropout rate and attendance rate as important indicators. For advanced students, we suggested tracking both the enrollment in advanced placement courses such as physics, calculus, and chemistry and the number of students scoring 450 or better on both the verbal and math sections of the SAT. It turns out that of 250,000 high school graduates in California every year, 100,000 take the SAT but only 41,000 score above 450 on the verbal section. This pool is where the doctors, lawyers, and professionals come from, and we wanted more kids to have a crack at those opportunities. So our goal became a statewide increase in the over-450 pool from 41,000 to 60,000 by 1990. As for the vast majority of students, we decided to look at the score on the California assessment test (which is administered yearly to all third, sixth, and twelfth graders), at the enrollment in selected academic courses, at the amount of homework given on a nightly basis, and at the frequency of writing assignments.

The initial reaction in the field was very hostile. I attended most of the regional meetings, and the same two arguments kept popping up. Some administrators said point blank that they just didn't like being measured. My response was that if we didn't establish the criteria for tracking school progress ourselves, somebody was going to do it for us—and probably not as well. So, I said, let's come up with professionally sound indices that push students in the right direction. School leaders bought that part, but the specific goals we had selected forced the issue of educational philosophy in California. Was the traditional curriculum really the best one for the average student? The criticism was, your indices are elitist; they only measure the college bound, they aren't relevant to the average student. I challenged that argument head-on. The whole thrust of the reform movement, I explained, is that the average student needs to take harder courses. The 75 percent of students who don't go to four-year colleges after graduation are precisely the ones most in need of the academic curriculum. The data from the Stanford Path study showed that it was this middle group that was being shortchanged in school, that was taking a very weak, incoherent course of studies, that was falling far short of its potential. These average students were the ones the schools had to start pushing once again.

After a long and healthy debate, we finally got agreement on that idea, too, and set some very ambitious academic targets. (The statewide targets have been established in three steps for the academic years 1985–86, 1987–88, and 1989–90.) For example, they include cutting the dropout rate by 20 percent, increasing the number of students taking physics by 40,000, and assuring that half the seniors do at least two hours of homework a night—all by the year 1990.

If the accountability program only operated at the statewide level, it probably wouldn't have been so controversial. After all, if the statewide goals aren't met, the logical person for the

✳

voters to hold responsible is the Superintendent of Public Instruction—yours truly—the fellow who dreamed them up. But accountability means accountability, and, significantly, California's plan also includes a local component. As part of the program, every school receives on an annual basis a profile of its performance, stating exactly how its students fared in each of the eight quality indices. There is also a section of the report in which local officials assess their record on such site-specific issues as the vitality and harmony of the school, the number of awards or recognitions that have been achieved, and any other indicators that they deem important. With regard to the numerical data, the results of the eight quality indices are tabulated alongside the school's marks from the previous year, the current statewide average, and, in the interests of fairness, the score from schools whose student bodies have similar socioeconomic backgrounds. (To derive this last set of figures, California's schools have been organized into comparison groups based on the education level and occupation of the students' parents— one of the best predictors of academic success.)

The advantages of, in effect, an annual rating of the performance of each of California's 7000 schools are notable. First, it galvanizes individual teachers, principals, and administrators to make the right structural changes—to emphasize academic courses, homework, and writing, for instance. Second, it respects the autonomy of the local school by allowing school leaders to set their own targets based on their own sense of what can be accomplished. Sacramento can't dictate that. Third, it helps parents by giving them up-to-date information on the performance of their child's school.

Matching the schools by comparison grouping is a diabolically clever thing to do, if I do say so myself. When I came to the Reed School District, it was a classic example of a school system that was coasting along on its socioeconomic laurels. Most of the students came from the well-heeled families of suburban Marin County. They were underachieving in terms of other school systems with comparable advantages, but their lack of accomplishment was disguised by the fact that their scores still exceeded the statewide average. Comparison grouping unmasks those schools that are failing to live up to their potential. On the other hand, it also spotlights the low socioeconomic schools that are getting the job done, and our data uncovered many inner city schools in California that are outperforming suburban schools in academic accomplishment. Under the terms of the California School Recognition Program, these models of exemplary achievement will be singled out for awards. In general, every school has been encouraged to set its quality targets so that by 1990 its ratings will be in the top quartile of its comparison group as determined by the 1983–84 base academic year. In this way, each school can compete with itself and with its peers, ratcheting the whole system upward over time toward the goal of academic excellence.

To be sure, the accountability program continues to have its detractors, educators who distrust systemwide goals, Sacramento-based leadership, standardized tests, and me (not necessarily in that order). Associate professor Larry Cuban of the Stanford School of Education took the accountability program to the woodshed in the editorial pages of the *San Jose Mercury News* on May 1, 1984. Accusing me of a "feverish worshipping of numbers" and of having "the mind of an auditor wedded to the heart of a lawyer," Cuban argued that teaching is "closer to carving a sculpture than making cars" and that the philistine notion of measuring school progress would result in a host of abuses, notably that teachers would be pressured to "cover content" instead of "cultivating critical thought" in their students.

I must admit, I don't follow the logic of someone who says that because schools are expected to cover course content that means they cannot cultivate the "higher-order" learning skills. Or, because the accountability program tracks such concrete data as dropout rates, SAT scores, and enrollment in academic courses, that means we are no longer interested in those transcendent functions, the development of good character, of loyalty to this democracy, and of individual growth, which we have already identified as the true purposes of education. Cuban goes astray, I think, with his insistence on the Cartesian logic of either/or. I have tried to emphasize in this book that learning is a seamless whole, that content and cultural literacy and the thinking skills and moral development tend to occur together. It isn't that we are interested in the data of the accountability program for their own sake. The numbers are surrogates. We record them and push for better results, because we have confidence that, if attendance improves and if more students are taking a solid academic curriculum, doing more homework, and completing more writing assignments, this traditional approach will conclude with the highest purposes of education being served as well.

We have had more or less of a struggle in the California legislature each year obtaining adequate school funding. This can be a decided headache, but there's been a silver lining to the cloud. Practically speaking, the struggle has kept educators who share Cuban's aversion to measurable goals pretty much in check. The basic terms of the bargain in California remain the same: more money for better results. And educators know it. In 1978, the Field Poll asked Californians whether spending more money for public education would improve the quality of the schools. Of those polled, 24 percent answered, "Yes, it would"; 57 percent answered, "no, it wouldn't." In 1983, the same question got the opposite response: 66 percent said yes, and 26 percent said no. This sea change in public confidence has come about because school officials have conscientiously cooperated with the reform effort at the local level. Districts whose attendees total 83 percent of the students in the state have adopted resolutions to examine such items as homework policies, discipline policies, course content, and the amount of writing expected and to bring about necessary improvements. In the end, these actions that penetrate to the classroom level are the ones that will determine whether the excellence agenda carries the day in California or not. In the next chapter, we examine these key local reform issues.

❈

PART TWO

The Excellence Agenda and You

CHAPTER SEVEN

Leverage Points for Reform

THE HEART and soul of a traditional education is the core curriculum of academic subjects. This core is the best way we know of cultivating those capacities in students—as workers, as citizens, and as private persons—that will enable them to take their place in society as productive, independent, and morally responsible adults. Important as the task of elevating the traditional disciplines to center stage is, however, that alone will not be sufficient to revitalize the public schools. Education is a cooperative venture. For the schools to become truly effective, hundreds of thousands of people— teachers and parents, principals and school board members, superintendents and the general public—will have to join the reform ranks and take part with a will. The remainder of this book focuses on how each of these groups can make an invaluable contribution to the excellence movement. First things first, however; in this chapter, we look at some shared responsibilities.

A number of unfortunate trends have plagued our schools since the seventies and need to be reversed. Specifically, the schools need to commit fully to the excitement of learning by buying better textbooks. They need to stand up for a discipline policy that unequivocally puts the interest of the majority of conscientious students ahead of the disposition to misbehave of a few bad ones. They need to stretch the students' time on task by assigning more homework. And they need a testing policy that rewards achievement and identifies patterns of underperformance so that those patterns can be eliminated. Archimedes said, "Give me a lever and a place to stand, and I'll move the earth." The four leverage points I have just listed— commonsense policies regarding textbooks, discipline, homework, and testing—are the tools with which the reform movement can move the public schools toward excellence. In this chapter, we investigate exactly what those policies are and how they can be achieved.

In one of his last official appearances, before the 1984 American Association of School Administrators' annual convention, Secretary of Education Terrel Bell criticized the "dumbing down" of U.S. textbooks. The phrase aptly describes the sorry state of affairs. In terms of vocabulary, sentence structure, and intellectual content, much of the material high school students encounter in their textbooks these days is considerably less challenging than a random page out of *Newsweek* or *The New York Times*. Textbooks for the first grade to the twelfth have been clipped, cropped, and polled of any distinguishing content, style, or point of view. Earlier I mentioned that while I was at Reed Union, we were forced to buy junior high school history books for our fifth-grade students because the reading levels of the popular series were pitched so low. This decline is no trivial matter. Studies have shown that, like it or not, textbooks are the basis for about 90 percent of what transpires in the classroom. Jeanne Chall's literacy research, which I have already recapped, found a direct correlation between the difficulty of the textbook series used and the eventual SAT scores of students: the harder the series, the higher the scores. The point is that if the text is resolutely simple-minded, it will be difficult for the quality of instruction to rise above it.

There are several reasons why intellectually impoverished textbooks have prospered in the public schools over the last twenty years. One pervasive problem is the fascination too many adopting committees have for something called the "readability formula." A readability formula is a method for mathematically assigning a level of reading difficulty to a given text. In general, the formulas involve counting the number of syllables in words and of words in sentences. If this approach seems arbitrary, it should. Readability formulas have resulted in such howlers as finding William Faulkner's *The Sound and the Fury* easy for children to read, but samples of their own writing too difficult. The formulas put a premium on short choppy sentences, limited vocabulary, homogenized tone, and watered-down content. If educators had sat down and tried to invent a method that positively guaranteed that students would be bored to tears by their textbooks, they could hardly have surpassed the net effect of the readability formulas.

Another element in the impoverishment of textbooks in the seventies was the attempt to edit content to meet the objections of special interests. Women and minorities had a legitimate point: our history and literature should avoid casual stereotypes and should present relevant role models for every child. Toward that end, many states, including California, adopted legal compliance codes for textbooks. But some textbook publishers nave interpreted these rules with a bureaucratic timidity that verges on the absurd. For instance, the men who signed the

Declaration of Independence and who have been known as the "founding fathers" to generations reemerged in several seventies' history textbooks as the "founders." An author whose children's story ended with a celebration in an ice cream parlor discovered her conclusion had been vetoed by the publisher, who feared the wrath of the nutrition lobby. Unfortunately, by the time textbooks had been edited to anticipate every objection, real or imagined, what was left just wasn't very interesting.

The final cause of textbook decline was the market itself— easy textbooks sold better than hard ones. Visual pyrotechnics and graphic glitz won out over content and substance. The reasons for this tilt were plain enough. In a typical class of thirty sixth graders, a teacher can expect a range of reading levels covering at least five grades. If a below-grade-level textbook is used to teach the subject of, say, geography, the students will have an easier time marching through the material (and the teacher will face fewer questions). This slow-down tactic enjoyed the ideological blessing of the seventies because the *Zeitgeist* of the schools was opposed to leaving anybody behind. But this benevolent approach was really killing our children with kindness. Educators have subsequently become more aware of what the average student misses when not asked to stretch. A weak textbook not only deprives children of information about the world, of a richer vocabularly, and of practice in making inferences, it also takes away the excitement of meeting new intellectual challenges.

I am far from feeling self-righteous on this whole topic because I remember falling into the glitz trap myself. I had just started teaching at Second Community and I decided to order a new math book. When I flipped through it, it looked really exciting. But using it to teach the next year, I discovered it was basically all smoke and mirrors. I paid the price for my mistake twice over. The first time, I had to scramble around until I acquired enough copies of an older math series to use in class. Believe me, I guarded those books like golden treasure. The second time was six years later when I had become superintendent of Reed. I called up the headquarters of the publisher to see if I could buy an updated version of that trusty old math book that had proved so effective. But a sales representative there told me they had just decided not to reissue that series again; they didn't think the market would absorb such a difficult book anymore. In a way, it was poetic justice—except the students were the ones who ended up being short-changed.

When I was appointed to the California Board of Education, I began raising the textbook issue at the state level. We had some hearings to air the matter. Mike Fallon, a reporter for the *Sacramento Union* and the dean of the California education press corps, called me up and asked me what the controversy was all about. I think I had the flu and I started giving him titles of old history textbooks that were out of print and of their current equivalents. "But, I'm a layman. I'll never understand what's different about them," he said. And I answered, "Michael, do me a favor. Go and read the books." Two days later, he rang me up again, absolutely incensed. He wrote a brilliant article quoting examples from the text—how gold was discovered in California according to a 1970 text and the same story in a 1980 version after the text had been "dumbed down." The difference between the exciting earlier account and the flat, uninflected, ho-hum tone of its replacement was like that between day and night. The story was picked up in newspapers around the country and was a turning point in bringing the issue to the public's attention.

As Mike Fallon learned, there's no great mystery about what makes a good or bad textbook. Adopting committees should keep in mind that what they are up to is always going to be more of an art than a science. In California, we have issued a set of criteria for textbook purchases that reflect the best advice of the nation's top experts. The criteria state our expectations as clearly as possible: we're looking for content-driven books that are engaging, that tell stories, that make the key points in the discipline but also go into depth on occasion, that have a coherent point of view, and that open up a field of thought and encourage further, independent reading. Clearly, for all the expertise backing them up, these criteria are also commonsense rules. The dominant concerns of adopting committees should always be the obvious ones: Is the book interesting? Is it informative? Is it well-written? Does it open up vistas? Reading difficulty is surely a consideration but not the overriding one. Worse things can happen to a student than having to look up a new word in a dictionary.

Thanks to the reform movement, the textbook market is starting to change. Over $1 billion is spent annually on textbooks in the United States. California accounts for 11 percent of that. New York and Florida make up another 12 percent. All three of these states have gone on record asking for tougher textbooks. Last year we held a conference in California sponsored by the Department of Education and the state's thirty largest school districts. Textbook experts, representatives from other states, and the major publishers were all there. We made the pitch for more challenging content. The publishers hemmed and hawed about readability formulas and compliance rules tying their hands, but I expect they will come around. Because as the reform movement takes hold, that's where the money will be. And, as I can attest, textbook publishers have highly sensitive antennae when it comes to anticipating the market.

At the original California hearings in 1977, I had been critical of the available history textbooks as being too abstract and lacking the vivid biographic detail necessary to involve kids in the drama of past events. "The Adams Chronicle" happened to be showing on public television at the time, and I suggested off the top of my head in one session that Abigail Adams would be a good person for students to know about. Sure enough, in 1982, when the new batch of history books came up for adoption, almost every single major publisher had an insert on Abigail Adams. (I wish I could have known what they were going to do. There were another couple of dozen American heroes I could have mentioned.) This incident suggests a couple of things to me. For one, change won't happen overnight. It takes four or five years, from conception through writing, editing, field-testing, and publishing, to prepare a new textbook for market. And for another, when textbook buyers talk, textbook publishers listen. It is up to the reform movement to make sure the message they hear is focused on excellence.

The second policy area that the reform movement needs to address is school discipline. Following a 1969 Supreme Court decision affirming that students do not "shed their Constitutional rights . . . at the schoolhouse gate," the dominant trend in the seventies, especially in large, urban public high schools, was the codification of students' "rights and responsibilities" into voluminous rule books. The general idea seemed to be that if an action wasn't explicitly forbidden, then it was permissible.

In the event of possible suspension or expulsion, the rule books outlined a whole quasi-judicial set of procedures to be followed. They included the student's right to a written notice of the charges, the right to an attorney, the right to cross-examine witnesses, the right to refuse to answer incriminating questions, the right to a transcript of the proceedings, and the right to an appeal. (All of which the school system paid for, of course.)

The chief sponsor of these changes was the American Civil Liberties Union, whose widely read paper "Academic Freedom in Secondary Schools" contained the model procedural language adopted by many school districts. The ACLU's intention was to replace what it called the "rule by personality" of school officials with a "rule by law" that explicitly defined the extent and limit of adult authority. The problem with taking the workings of civil law and procedure as the model for school discipline is that this model is unwieldly and inappropriate. The tone of the school quickly becomes pegged at what is legally permissible instead of what is desirable or proper. If the goal of education is the formation of good character (as we have been arguing), the standard of what will hold up in court is not high enough. As Justice Frankfurter put it, "Much that is legally permitted is repugnant to the civilized mind." A larger, consensual spirit of civilized morality should obtain in the school setting, and the principal and faculty should be afforded the discretionary power they need to uphold that standard. The last thing adolescents need in their quest to attach to the values of society is the spectacle of adult authority hamstrung by a raft of procedural folderol. We're not training future felons in the subtleties of playing the system; we're educating adolescents. Indeed, research on school effectiveness shows that an orderly atmosphere is one of the hallmarks of a successful school.

＊

On the other hand, a good example of how not to instill order was published in the *San Francisco Examiner* at the beginning of the 1984 school year. An Alameda teacher sent home with her sixth-grade students a list of "essential behaviors" for parents to read and sign. The shortened version published by the newspaper contained over 100 prohibitions, including "no gawking through either side of any window," "no excessive or repetitious pencil sharpening," and "no pouting, petulance, pestiness, ill will, mutiny, uncooperation, impoliteness, insubordination . . . etc." This glut of negatives virtually guaranteed that all of the commands would be ignored. In my opinion, beyond a few firm housekeeping rules, all that students really need to hear in a disciplinary code are a few basic precepts: something like "School is a place for learning. Take advantage of the opportunity, and respect the right of your classmates to do so as well." The idea is to foster an ethos of mutual respect and trust. That is best accomplished when teachers behave as models of courtesy and, in turn, expect a reciprocal courtesy from their students. Consistency in enforcement and high expectations are the keys. When a student violates civilized norms—whether by throwing food in the cafeteria, cheating on an exam, or selling marijuana—good teachers never look the other way. They act. And school administrators respond quickly, fairly, and in proportion to the seriousness of the offense.

Although violence, vandalism, and drug use get the headlines, these are not the discipline problems that most bother teachers. In polls, teachers are far more likely to complain about students "talking out in class," "failing to bring books," or "not paying attention." These symptoms of resistance to the hard work of learning are more or less inevitable in isolated cases. The main thing is that they not be allowed to become endemic. A good curriculum, dedicated faculty, and a school-wide sense of seriousness about education are the most effective antidotes.

There is a small, hard core of emotionally disturbed or even criminal youngsters whose capacity to disrupt the learning environment, if they are allowed to do so, vastly exceeds their number. In these cases, even if it means going through an expensive and time-consuming process, the principal must seek the remedy of suspension or expulsion. The justification for taking such a step is twofold. First, the right of the majority of students to learn obviously outweighs the right of the individual to disrupt. And second, expulsion is hardly tantamount to capital punishment. Our society offers many second chances. The student can always transfer to a private school or to another public school district, or (under California law, for example) wait out the sentence and start afresh at the beginning of the next semester (perhaps even a little wiser for the wear).

The indications look good that the requisite climate of stability that marks successful schools can be restored in the public system. The 1985 Supreme Court ruling on *New Jersey* vs. *T.L.O.* explicitly affirmed that school officials may search a student without a warrant when they have reasonable grounds to believe that a school rule may have been violated. The Court thus recognized that educators enjoy a certain privilege in discharging their responsibility to safeguard the learning environment. This decision strikes the proper balance between the rights of the student as an individual and the rights of the student body as a whole. More importantly, it gives the necessary signal to school leaders that maintaining order on campus is constitutional, too.

The third leverage point for reform is a sound homework

✳

policy. Homework is the cheapest, most cost-effective way for an education system to prolong the school day. In a recent review of the research, Herbert Walberg maintains that homework turns out to be one of the most powerful ways to improve student performance, especially if graded or integrated into classroom work. It not only increases the student's time on task at little or no public expense, it provides a qualitatively different—and in some ways, superior—experience. All real learning is active. A good homework assignment requires the student to solve problems, to compose paragraphs, to test his or her own mettle, and to think. Too often, homework becomes exclusively fill-in-the-blank, workbook-type assignments. There's a place for those exercises in learning spelling or grammar. But there's also a place for more challenging possibilities such as book reports on independent reading, kitchen-counter science experiments, and math puzzles. Homework that engages the student's intellect teaches self-reliance in a way classroom activities by themselves never could. Finally, when teachers insist that homework be turned in on time, they teach a crucial lesson on how to succeed in life after graduation.

Despite all these advantages, however, homework fell out of fashion in the seventies. A survey by the California Department of Education in 1979 revealed that a third of all sixth-grade pupils did no homework whatsoever, and over a six-week period, a quarter of high school seniors hadn't received a single writing assignment. As the reform movement has taken hold, this situation has been improving. By their own report, California's sixth graders are now averaging a half-hour more per night on their homework than they did in 1979. And the state goal for high school students is that half of them will be studying two hours a night by 1990.

The fourth, and final, leverage point for reform concerns the use of tests. In the seventies, standardized tests were treated like the messenger who brought tidings of military defeat to the King of Persia. Both messenger and tests were held responsible for the bad news they reported. Year after year, as the SAT scores slipped another notch or two, education lobbying groups would find another reason to protest: the SAT tests are discriminatory against minority and low-income students; they only measure a narrow set of cognitive "tricks"; they are psychologically damaging to students who don't do well. Terry Herndon, who at the time was president of the nation's largest teachers' union, the National Education Association, said that the SAT and other college entrance exams "maim in equally harsh ways more people than do Detroit cars" and called for their abolition.

Of course, no tests, no more bad news about falling scores, right? I think the standardized tests can be useful tools, not just for the college bound in high school but at every level of schooling. The difficulty right now is that the standardized tests that are commonly administered by states are too narrowly focused on basic skills and minimum competencies. The states should raise their sights. I would like to see elementary, junior high, and high school exams that tested for achievement and content. Students of English literature ought to be able to answer questions about *Hamlet* and *Moby Dick* by the time they graduate. Chemistry students ought to be able to explain the properties of elements in terms of the atomic arrangement of electrons, protons, and neutrons. Students of world history ought to know the significance of the Battle of Waterloo. Standardized tests given as final exams would function as measures of what the students actually learned and therefore would have the salutary effect of certifying the integrity of the course.

The danger of relying too heavily on such exams, of course, is that teachers will begin aiming their courses exclusively at the tests. They might be tempted to gallop through an encyclopedia of facts and slight the development of problem-solving skills and independent inquiry—as has happened in Japan. The protection against this eventuality is to tailor the exams so they measure the full range of higher-order academic skills. California has recently launched the Golden State Exams to do just that.

Looking into the future, I foresee an expanded role for standardized tests, in systemwide quality control and in diagnosing strengths and weaknesses. A technological breakthrough, the power of the computer to process mountains of data quickly and cheaply, virtually guarantees this outcome. We are just beginning to learn how to exploit this new tool. For instance, even though students continually move in and out, we can now make better class-by-class or school-by-school comparisons by using computers to reassemble the original cohort. Through the use of computers we can also now report to California high schools how their graduates are doing in their first year at the University of California or California State University on a campus-by-campus, grade-point-average basis. This kind of information is useful for decision makers because it helps them understand what is working in the schools and what is not.

Now that the four leverage points for school reform—tougher textbooks, discipline, homework, and testing—have been identified, the question that remains is how they are to be achieved. We can't just issue an edict. If the last quarter of a century of failed revolutions in the educational arena have proved anything, critics justly point out, it is that "top-down" reform doesn't work. On the other hand, anarchy isn't a very inviting alternative either. For reform to take hold, the people in the trenches—the teachers and principals and school staff—have to commit themselves, and so do policy makers at the district and state levels.

Textbooks are a perfect example of this interdependence. In California, the money to buy new elementary and junior high textbooks is appropriated by the legislature. The state board of education issues criteria to publishers and approves for purchase those books that meet its specifications. The large local districts have their own set of experts, adoption committees, and approval lists. Ultimately, the teacher has to choose among the few available alternatives that have filtered down through all the upper levels. The point is obvious. Better textbooks will actually make it into the hands of students only if the whole blessed education apparatus cooperates. And the same can be said of discipline. A heroic teacher battling the odds in an out-of-control school will find it next to impossible to create a climate of order and academic purpose singlehandedly. But a faculty working together under the leadership of a determined principal can. Ditto homework: one teacher can be brushed aside; a whole faculty raising the roof cannot. The cumulative effect in education is always greater than the sum of the parts. That's why it's time for educators at all levels to put aside the ancient turf rivalries and recognize the truth of the matter: we're all in this thing together. For excellence to prevail, each of the levels of the public school system has to reform itself because each is indispensable to the right functioning of the rest and to the only acceptable outcome—the best education possible for every student.

We begin our survey of how the reform agenda is to be implemented with a look at the key player at the site level—the school principal. Good principals are natural leaders. They know how to articulate the underlying values and purposes of the school and to get students and teachers to strive toward those goals as a team. A good principal is like the captain of a ship—he or she knows where the vessel is headed and what it will take to get there.

Reuben Trinidad personifies these traits. When he stepped in as principal of Overfelt High School in 1982, the predominantly Hispanic school in East San Jose had graffiti all over its walls, high absenteeism, gang fights, and a rampant drug problem. The campus wasn't a safe place to be, much less to study, so Trinidad made discipline his top priority. Lockers were sealed to get rid of hiding places for weapons and drugs as well as to eliminate the prime excuse for loitering in the halls. Radios, smoking, and club jackets were banned. The campus was "closed"; that is, leaving or entering during the day without special permission was prohibited. With Trinidad's encouragement, teachers cracked down on foul language, tardiness, and class disruptions. Parents were called in (and picked up at home when necessary) to discuss their children's behavior. Detentions and suspensions were routinely handed out.

Knocking on doors in the neighborhood on Saturday mornings, Trinidad asked the community to pitch in on a school face-lift. In the summer of 1983, sixty-two parents, fourteen staff members and twenty-seven students spent nine weeks repainting the school building beige with chocolate trim. Absenteeism declined by a third; academic performance picked up (Overfelt recently won first place in a math field day competition); and in 1985, the school was singled out for national recognition by the Justice Department as a "turnaround school."

A principal's strong leadership made the dramatic difference at Overfelt, but in less obvious ways, a strong principal makes the difference in every outstanding school. The principal is the instructional leader. That means he or she guides the academic program by fine-tuning the curriculum, by checking the performance of teachers and helping them to improve, and by communicating schoolwide expectations with regard to homework policy, discipline, academic achievement, and values. In too many schools, the principal functions as a glorified groundskeeper, turning the lights off at the end of a day and seeing to it that the lawn gets mowed. That's not enough. The vital task of the principal is convincing the staff to work together in a common direction, transforming a group of individuals into a faculty, and building *espirit de corps*. That requires finding out what's going on, getting out of the office and into the classroom, providing instructional leadership. People need to feel that they are part of a project with worthwhile goals, direction, and purpose. Only the principal can provide that leadership to the school community—and the best ones do.

In the educational chain of command, the principal reports to the school district office. A school district is an administrative unit consisting of any number of schools, from a handful to several hundred. It is run on a day-to-day basis by a superintendent and staff and on a policy basis by an elected school board. The school district is especially well situated to handle certain reform tasks, for instance, building a rapport with community and business leaders so that they are aware of and support what's going on at the local schools. It also provides guidance in areas such as homework policy, discipline, curriculum, and staff development. Without doubt, however, the most effective measure that the school district can take to improve the quality of education is to hire good principals—and then hold them accountable.

Too many school boards spend most of their time on budgets and buildings and not enough on the whole purpose of the enterprise. How much writing are the students doing each week? How much homework and of what quality? Are the teachers being observed and helped to become more effective at their craft? What's the learning atmosphere at each school? How do we know? Clearly, if the principal is the one holding the bag for a school's success or failure, he or she should also be given the autonomy necessary to do the job. The principal should have a strong say in the hiring—and absolute say in the firing— of teachers, as well as discretionary control over as much of the school budget as possible.

School district offices are an easy target for critics convinced that nothing worthwhile takes place in them. But the fact is that strong leadership from the district office is an essential ingredient of school reform. Superintendents like Harry Handler of Los Angeles, who called fifty principals on the carpet when he wasn't satisfied with the state of affairs in their schools; or Ray Cortines of San Jose, whose high academic expectations have infused a "new atmosphere of hope," to use the words of the same Stanford researcher who five years ago made national news by describing the district's oldest high school in an article titled "The Death of a High School;" or Tom Payzant of San Diego; or Ed Dundon of Garden Grove; or Fred Stewart of San Juan; or John Stemple of Fresno, or Jake Abbot of Mt. Diablo; or Gene Tucker of ABC or Bob Alioto of San Francisco—all of these outstanding individuals have set a tone in their districts that breeds success and better classroom performance.

A state's department of education operates at yet one more remove from the focus of learning, which is the student. Its reform role is accordingly more general: to provide broad leadership on such issues as graduation requirements, academic goals, textbook choice, and testing for accountability. The rallying cry of public education used to be "local control," meaning that the local districts ran the show as they saw fit. That made sense back when school funding was also a local affair. But California's Proposition 13, which curtailed school reliance on the local property tax, and the many parallel laws subsequently passed in states around the country changed all that. Now most of the money for schools comes from state treasuries and the legislatures have a direct stake in making sure the taxpayers' money is being well spent. Thus, the states' increasing involvement in accountability, via standardized tests and the other indices listed in Chapter Six.

The trick for any state is to somehow push systemwide accountability without thwarting local initiative, especially the discretionary power of the principal to react to on-site circumstances and opportunities. This balance can be struck, but it's not going to be easy. It goes against the grain of a bureaucracy to relinquish power. When I became state superintendent, I cut the state-financed budget of the Department of Education from $31 million to $25 million and, through attrition and early retirement, reduced the work force by 15 percent. The only discernible effect was that information from the field started reaching me quicker. The point is that both state and district offices must exercise bureaucratic self-control. At the heart of the problem, there's an organizational paradox. The money in public education comes largely from the legislature, but the learning takes place in the classroom. Financing is top-down, if you will, but the real action in the schools must come from the bottom up. The solution is to wed local autonomy to accountability. The public school system should take a page out of contemporary business literature. In books like *In Search of Excellence,* the secret of successful management is described in terms of developing an organizationwide consensus about goals, then letting the local units decide how those goals are to be met, and watching the bottom line. To the degree that we follow that prescription in the public school system, I think the excellence movement will prevail.

That is, it will prevail providing—as I keep saying—that enough people put their shoulders to the wheel. So far, I haven't mentioned the reform role of the single largest group of professional educators, the teachers. Education reform without their support would be like Normandy Beach without the landing craft—a nonevent. It is they who command the classroom. It is they who are charged with educating our children on a day-to-day basis. And it is they who will make or break the excellence movement. In the next chapter, we consider the role of the teacher in school reform.

CHAPTER EIGHT

Rallying the Teachers

IN JULY of 1983, the American Federation of Teachers held its annual convention in Los Angeles and invited me to address the group. California was in the midst of adopting an omnibus school reform and funding package at the time. Among other things, the final bill (which the pundits had said could never be passed) shuttled an extra $850 million to the public schools—most of it destined to end up in the pockets of California's teachers. That, along with my background in education as a public school teacher, might have occasioned a rousing welcome in a Hollywood script. But a disconcerting thing happened when I stood up to speak. Scattered members of the audience began to hiss. And as I got to the part in the speech where I explained the new mentor-teacher concept, which allowed for an extra $4000 per year for outstanding teachers who took on additional duties, the hisses turned to boos. When I was done, Albert Shanker, the president of the federation, who had invited me because of his interest in school reform, asked the delegates to please refrain from hooting down the speakers.

Clearly, a reputation for being "antiteacher" had preceded me to the convention floor. But what had I done to earn it?

The answer is that I had transgressed one of the guild rules. During my campaign for the office of Superintendent of Public Instruction, I had been so bold as to say out loud what everyone who has ever worked in a public school knows to be the truth: that 5 to 10 percent of the teachers in the system are incompetent and that current legal procedures make it too difficult to get rid of them.

Let me hasten to add: I am not one of your chronic teacher-bashers who is only too ready, willing, and able to lay all the ills of the public schools at the doorstep of poor instruction. I sincerely believe that teaching is a noble profession, that undertaking to enlighten the minds and spirits of children is one of the highest vocations an individual can aspire to, and that teachers generally measure up. Most of the teachers I have worked with in the public schools have been conscientious and competent; a few have been brilliant; and a handful just plain didn't belong in the classroom. Does saying that make me "anti-teacher"? I don't think so. If one surgeon brought malpractice charges against another on the grounds of habitual drunkenness, no one would even suggest the former was "antidoctor."

According to the Gallup Poll, when asked to rate the contribution various professions make to society, the U.S. public puts school teachers high on the list—third only to physicians and the clergy. That's a flattering appraisal, but I wonder how long it can last. Considerably farther down the list of public esteem comes the profession of lawyer, my occupation before I retooled as a teacher. One thing about lawyers, however: they have a very clear ethical mandate to uphold the standards of the bar. Teachers' organizations, on the other hand, historically have acted on the premise that the job security of their members is more important than the reputation of the profession.

As a brief example, shortly after I took office, a new law went into effect mandating that new teachers must pass a basic-skills test in mathematics, English usage, and writing before being certified in California. The law was sponsored by Gary Hart, at the time an assemblyman (and no relation to the Senator from Colorado). Leaders of the California Teachers Association opposed it because they were afraid the competency test requirement might eventually be extended to all teachers, thus threatening job security. In fact, they were so irritated at Hart's brainchild that when he ran for the state senate in 1982 they endorsed and financially backed his opponent. (Hart won anyway.)

Despite this opposition, in February of 1983, we began administering the California Basic Educational Skills Test to all new teacher candidates. The test was indeed basic. A math question might require that you know that the perimeter of a figure is equal to the sum of the lengths of its sides. The reading section focused on finding the main idea in 200-word-long paragraphs. Marilyn Bittle, the president of the California Teachers Association and a member of the advisory group that okayed the test, said that any competent high school student should be able to pass it. Nevertheless, in the first year, 31 percent of the teacher candidates—freshly graduated from collegiate schools of education—failed CBEST. Obviously, the test had been needed all along.

In my opinion, the substantial majority of the teacher corps is a credit to the profession. But that should be all the more incentive to go after those who don't measure up. The excellence movement doesn't contend that only intellectual and moral superhumans can make the schools work or should be allowed to teach—far from it. The qualities that mark a good teacher, as Dr. Ernest L. Boyer, president of the Carnegie Foundation, has written, are so old-fashioned and familiar that it's almost an embarrassment to list them. I cannot improve on Ernie Boyer's level-headed definition. Very simply, it is that a good teacher is a person who loves the subject matter and knows it inside out, who believes in the potential of every student to learn and won't take "no" for an answer, and, finally, who has the human ability—the warmth, the caring, the integrity—to reach children and make them come alive as students.

It bears repeating; the foundation of a good teacher is a love of learning. A survey was done among California children and this question was posed: "What do you want in a teacher?" The most frequent response was "I want the teacher to know the subject matter." Especially in the upper-elementary grades, kids are natural intellectuals. They're curious. They want to know how things work and how they got that way. They want to be with somebody who understands the subject matter in depth and who has the contagious enthusiasm to get it across. That, combined with high standards and a sincere interest in each child, makes a crackerjack teacher.

The reality of the situation, however, is that too many new teachers miss out on the very first qualification: they are not academically inclined. A study of students at more than 1000 colleges that reviewed performance in nineteen subject majors found that potential teachers ranked fourteenth in English and seventeenth in math, ahead of only the industrial arts and home economics majors. Over the last decade, the SAT scores for prospective teachers fell about twice as fast as the average decline. This deterioration in quality reflects a drying up of the pool of interested college students. In 1966, a quarter of all college students said they would consider teaching as a career; today, fewer than 4 percent say so.

Why has this happened? Part of the problem is actually a by-product of general social progress: the schools lost their supply of indentured talent. As job opportunities have opened up for women in business, law, and medicine, fewer of them have been choosing what used to be one of the few career options available to them—teaching. In 1976, 100,000 fewer women majored in education than did in 1966.

The other main problem has been money. Even making allowance for the long summer vacation, teachers start out earning substantially less than individuals holding jobs requiring comparable training or, for that matter, no training at all. A new teacher in California in 1982 could expect to earn $13,500 a year, or about $5,000 less than a new toll collector on the Golden Gate Bridge. Furthermore, since the salary structure of teachers tends to be flat, the gap widens over time. After twenty years on the job, a teacher with a master's degree in education is making $25,000 less per year than an individual with a master's degree and comparable experience who is working in an industrial setting. These salary discrepancies have led to some serious shortages. In 1982, five times as many math teachers quit their jobs in California as retired. New ones are needed in the thousands, but in 1982, the California State University and the University of California systems together graduated only ninety-seven candidates. "The problem," a Marin County school board member drily remarked to me, "is that math teachers can count."

It isn't merely a matter of money, however. Ten times as many graduates of the University of California at Berkeley are going into the Peace Corps and Vista as are going into teaching. According to the *Los Angeles Times,* parochial school teachers in that city make half of what public school teachers do, but their students score better in national tests and they express greater job satisfaction. Teachers aren't like stockbrokers or auto mechanics. You will never understand the profession until you concede a quirky truth: most teachers got involved in the schools in the first place because they love what they do; they feel a sense of mission. They should be paid a decent wage, of course, because they are professionals. But that's not all that matters to them. They also value the psychic rewards of bringing out the best in children, of educating them. That was certainly my own experience—I was a lawyer, got hooked on teaching, and became a teacher. I've never regretted that. But, more and more, individuals within the profession do. In 1971, 13 percent of high school teachers said they "probably" would not go into teaching if they had it to do over again; by 1981, that index of dissatisfaction had tripled. The sources of teachers' frustration are myriad, but study after study identifies several common complaints. The psychic rewards keep getting harder to find. Children have always been difficult, but these days they seem less motivated to learn, less likely to express their gratitude for a job well done. And the profession is isolating; teachers are consigned to a classroom all day by a heavy schedule and are unable to consult with other adults or to renew themselves professionally.

These are the kinds of problems that the reform agenda must address if we are going to rally the teaching profession to the excellence banner. The scope of the challenge is enormous. In California alone, we need to locate 110,000 new teachers by 1991. (There are only 170,000 in the system right now.) The echo of the baby boom is on its way; the California public school system projects its enrollment will increase from 4,100,000 to 4,700,000 by 1991. The new wave of children has already been born. Where will we find enough competent, committed, and caring teachers to handle them?

To start with, I think we have to go out and actively recruit the best and the brightest. The way to do that is to compete on the merits. We have to remind young people of the crucial importance of the teaching profession for our economy, our democracy, and the moral tenor of our society. We have to point out that because teaching is intimately concerned with the growth and development of the next generation, it is inherently meaningful work. And we can't be shy about out message. I have been going to campuses, talking to college students, taking along some of our best mentor teachers, and trying to convey how interesting teaching can be. We are setting up "future teacher" clubs in our high schools again—something that hasn't been seen in California in twenty years. We have taped and released public service spots for television using the tag line "Take responsibility for a new generation."

Last but not least, we've raised the financial stakes. Teaching is an important profession, and one way our society tells people what is important is with money. In California, we have boosted a starting teacher's salary 30 percent in the last three years to $20,000. At that level, the schools can now at least compete with business and industry for the top talent. And we're seeing the results. Enrollment at California State University campuses, which graduate 10 percent of the teachers in the United States, is up. And at the prestigious Stanford School of Education, applications have more than doubled.

Once the better candidates start coming through the door,

the next step is to upgrade the quality of the training they receive at the schools of education. Even that statement simplifies the problem a bit. In California, for instance, the schools of education only have the teacher trainees for 20 percent of their college careers, and half of that time is dedicated to student teaching. Obviously, then, readying an individual to become the ambassador of adult culture to a classroom full of youngsters has to be a campuswide undertaking. The starting point is clear. To do their job well, novice teachers need a broad, college-level liberal arts background, a solid grounding in the humanities, sciences, and mathematics. Second, they also have to learn something called "subject matter competency." It's not enough to know the scientific principles if you want to teach science; you also have to know how to package the ideas so you can get them across to a group of fifth graders—which is an entirely different proposition. In their impatience and zeal, some critics have called for the virtual abolition of all schools of education, which they see as irredeemable black holes of procedural stultification. I disagree. There are eminently practical tasks for schools of education to discharge. In learning multiplication or division, for instance, there are common mistakes or error patterns that children are going to fall into— that's guaranteed. And if you know what those are, as a teacher, you can do something about them. Getting that kind of concrete, useable information to teacher trainees will require an organized effort at the university level. It will require that the deans of education and the other department faculties sit down around a table and work out who does what. What are the key ideas to get across in teaching the history of the United States? How do you tailor a course in introductory biology? These questions are now being asked in California and in the rest of

✳

the country. Schools of education are willing to change, but they will need assistance from the whole university to train better teachers.

Right now, when novice teachers arrive at their first assignments, they're faced more or less with a sink-or-swim proposition. The newcomers either cope or don't; and, even if they do, after a few years they may look up and see the future looming ahead as a grim, gray, thirty-year march toward retirement. The unfortunate result is that we lose half of our teachers in their first six years on the job, and statistics show that those with the best academic records are the ones most likely to depart. We need to break this alarming pattern of attrition and hold on to more of our topflight people. We can accomplish both of these goals by widely adopting another item on the reform agenda—the career ladder.

Tennessee and Florida have been leaders in this area. Basically, the career ladder offers an alternative pattern of advancement so that those teachers who love to teach can stay in the classroom, take on more responsibility, and make progress without moving into administration. Here's how it works. Beginning teachers enter schools as apprentices (not unlike medical residents in a hospital). During a probationary period lasting a couple of years, they are teamed with the best teachers in the school, who regularly observe their classes, give tips on what needs work, and serve as resources. Upon completion of this period, each apprentice is tenured and has the option of pursuing the next level of attainment (just as a public accountant has the option of becoming a certified public accountant). Achieving senior teacher status requires passing a test given by a board of examiners that documents both a high level of knowledge of subject matter and an expertise in teaching it.

The teachers who elect to follow this route also follow a fast track up the pay scale—while getting to stay in the classroom. The next step is to become a master teacher. At this level, the teachers have an adjusted classroom load so that they can take on increased responsibilities for coaching new faculty members and for curriculum improvement.

In California, we passed a modified version of this plan, giving an additional $4000 to up to 5 percent of a district's teachers, who are selected because of their outstanding talent. These mentor teachers receive the stipend for three years and in return must spend at least 60 percent of their time in the classroom. The rest of the time they help out new teachers or work on curriculum development. I happened to meet a new mentor teacher in the San Juan School District (a large, suburban district outside Sacramento). He taught physics and for the first time in twenty years, he told me, he was sitting down with other physics teachers in the district and swapping notes and ideas. How do you teach the concept of mass? What demonstrations really bring the idea across? In Japan, teachers work a longer school year—220 days—but a full third of their time is spent in collaboration with peers on how to improve the quality of what they teach. We have got to make a comparable investment in our teachers, both to break down the sense of isolation they feel and to get the staff working together in a common direction. That's what creates school spirit and what successful schools have—a faculty concerned about the climate of the school and working together to improve it.

As teachers gain more recognition as professionals, however, it would behoove them to look deep within their ranks and ask some hard questions. One of the traditional hallmarks of any profession is that it polices itself. In the past, teachers' unions have taken the position, and very effectively translated it into labor contracts, that their major obligation is to protect the job of anyone carrying a union card. From an historical viewpoint, this hard-nosed bargaining for due process makes sense. Once upon a time, male administrators gratuitously fired female teachers for the awful crime of getting married. So the teachers did the logical thing; they formed a union to protect themselves against such arbitrary decisions. Now, however, the pendulum has swung to the opposite extreme. In California, firing an incompetent teacher takes at least a couple of years of administrative effort and costs upwards of $70,000. Before the omnibus reform bill passed in 1983, tenure reviews were frequently thrown out of administrative court because some subcodicil of the elaborate discharge protocol had been inadvertently missed by the school district. As I traveled around the state during the campaign, the most common complaint I heard from parents was that their child was being taught by an incompetent, someone incapable of uttering a grammatically correct sentence or, worse yet, someone habitually inebriated, but whom the school wouldn't replace. When I talked to school board members, however, they put it this way: "Look, Bill, the only way you're going to get rid of a tenured teacher these days is if he's a convicted child molester."

That's an exaggeration, but just barely. Many teachers recognize the problem. An eclectic cross section of California educators—teachers, university people, school administrators, and so on—were meeting at the state's oceanfront retreat at Asilomar for a weekend of brainstorming about the professionalization of teaching. We broke into small groups of ten, and one of the teachers in my group made a startling observation. She had been a nurse before she began teaching, she said, and the main difference she noticed was the absence of the idea of craft. "In nursing, everybody was clear about what was a fine piece of work," she said. "If a nurse fell below that standard, everyone else would be on her case right away." But teaching wasn't like that. "In the first place, there's not the agreement on what's good practice. But even more of a deterrent is the fact that if you pop off about somebody falling short, it's deeply resented. You're frozen out. There's not a willingness to hold oneself and each other up to a common set of standards."

That has to change. Teachers need to start defining the interests of their profession in more visionary terms than the us-against-them mind-set of the Industrial Revolution. They need to shed the more tendentious aspects of unionism. (I don't know how else to describe the group of teachers who demanded a pay raise from their district to cover continuing education after taking a college course on improving their collective bargaining negotiation skills.) The National Education Association—with 1,600,000 members, the largest teachers' union in the United States—has opposed the education reform movement from the outset. Before the national reports came out, the NEA hired the J. Walter Thompson advertising agency to spread the public relations word that everything was just fine in U.S. education, thank you—except for the lack of money. After the reports hit, the NEA announced its opposition to most of the remedies proposed. The union response staked out positions against "rigid graduation requirements," against an academic curriculum that would "cause students to drop out or be pushed out," against standardized tests, and against merit pay for outstanding teachers.

Fortunately, the evidence is that the NEA is out of step with its own membership. The Harris Poll assayed teacher opinion in the summer of 1984, and, point by point, found overwhelming support for the reform agenda. By 91 percent to 8 percent, teachers supported tighter graduation requirements, including more emphasis on academic subjects; by 74 percent to 24 percent, they favored increasing homework at every level; by 87 percent to 12 percent, they supported the concept of career ladders; and by 84 percent to 12 percent, they backed changes that would make it easier to remove incompetent teachers. Incidentally, a virtually unanimous 96 percent endorsed the sentiment "I love to teach."

In California, we have a good, constructive relationship with the teachers' organizations. Marilyn Bittle, the president of the California Teachers Association, Raoul Teilheit, the president of the California Federation of Teachers, and I meet with representatives of other major education organizations on a regular basis to talk about how best to prepare the next generation of teachers. This close contact, and the occasional follow-up phone call, has helped prevent misunderstandings in several school districts from becoming serious problems. Nationwide, the American Federation of Teachers and its president, Albert Shanker, have taken a statesmanlike position on the reform agenda. Shanker has become one of the country's leading advocates of educational excellence and improved professional standards. Another hopeful sign is that just recently, the NEA, at its national convention, adopted a more forceful stand in support of dealing with teacher incompetency and testing of prospective teachers. The last time the United States had an academic renaissance—after the orbiting of *Sputnik*—the emphasis was on teaching machines and the development of "teacher-proof" curricula. As Al Shanker points out, back then "teacher-proof" was a code word for "foolproof." This time, the excellence movement recognizes that the enthusiastic support of the existing cadre of teachers is indispensable to the success of the public school system.

Teachers are professionals. Each day in the classroom, they make creative decisions about how to package the lesson, how to allocate time, how to stucture activities, what facts to communicate, what skills to coach, and what discussions and trains of thought to set rolling. There's nothing else quite like teaching in the world. The reform agenda merely issues a timely reminder: along with the privileges of the profession comes the responsibility to defend its integrity.

CHAPTER NINE

How Parents Can Help

T HE MOST influential teachers in a student's life aren't the ones standing at the head of the class. In terms of a child's self-image and attitudes about achievement and the value of learning, the first and longest-lasting lessons are those imparted by the parents. Parents create the conditions at home that make children want to learn at school. They also can serve as an effective goad to sound educational practice at the local level and—once they have been organized *en masse*— as an unstoppable force for better schools in state politics. In short, parental involvement is as essential to the ultimate success of the school reform movement as a well-tended mainspring is to the right functioning of a Swiss pocket watch. In this chapter, we examine the excellence agenda from the practical standpoint of how parents can help.

The evidence all points in the same direction: the most important way in which parents can contribute to the education of their children is by what they do at home. Herbert Walberg and others have studied home environments thoroughly and identified some key elements that correlate well with success at school. We intuitively think of money or social class as significant advantages in learning, and they are. But Walberg's research shows that the general health of the family unit itself is even more important. In fact, a series of commonsense steps that any parent can take is twice as powerful as socioeconomic class in predicting which child will succeed in school. Specifically, the children who typically perform better in school are the children of parents who read to them when they are young, who supervise their homework by making sure they have a quiet place to study, who talk with them about school and everyday events and express an interest in their progress, who take them to parks, museums, ballgames, libraries, zoos, and other stimulating places, and who establish a definite, routine bedtime. It seems that the traditional hallmarks of a wholesome family life set the stage for academic achievement.

I don't think this revelation will astonish anyone. And I realize that a book such as this one is, to a large degree, self-selecting. Those parents who read it are likely to be those who already do such obvious things as encouraging their children to excel academically. How then do we reach the parents who aren't so conscientious or who may need reminding? According to a Gallup Poll in 1984, when asked what the biggest problem facing the public schools was, teachers ranked "lack of parental involvement" at the very top. Educators have been pointing the finger of blame at parents for the decline in school performance for a long time. Unfortunately, the next thing they do is throw up their hands and say, "That's out of our control." But, if we're serious about improving the schools, long-suffering resignation is not the answer. There's a great deal we all can do to encourage good parenting. Because it recognizes that enlisting help from the home front is crucial to the success of the education enterprise, the public school reform movement is setting out to do just that.

In California, we launched a major public service campaign at no cost to the taxpayer. Safeway printed our motto, "Parents are Teachers, Too," on grocery bags, and dairies put the message on milk cartons. Four corporations, Bank of America, Chevron, Arco, and First Interstate, paid for the development of TV and radio spots. We had a nice song, and the spots showed parents "teaching" their children by praising a good report card, reading the newspaper comics with them, or just spending time with them and being affectionate. It's not technical expertise that matters; it's that the child see that learning is valued and important in the eyes of adults. We printed 2,200,000 pamphlets carrying this message (250,000 of them in Spanish), jointly organized "parent education programs" with the school districts, and held a series of rallies around the state. At the rallies, we had children's choruses singing, lots of U.S. flags, and huge turnouts. Parents were asked to sign a pledge committing themselves to spend a half-hour of quality time every night—with the television, radio, telephone, and stereo unplugged—reading to or talking with their kids. We ended up with over 100,000 parents taking the pledge.

The issue of television watching is worth a few words here. When viewed in moderation, television can be a genuine addition to the education of any child. The fact is, however, that left to their own devices, the viewing habits of most children won't be moderate; more likely, they'll quickly approach the obsessive. The average sixth grader spends more hours in front of a TV set than in a classroom. For young "couch potatoes," planted in front of the tube four and five hours a day, TV programming isn't the alternative curriculum; school is.

That's not healthy. Every parent should be aware of the likely consequences. The fact is that academic achievement and time spent viewing television are inversely related. The results of the California Achievement Test given at the sixth, eighth, and twelfth grades are consistent. The more television a child reports watching, the lower his or her reading scores and verbal skills are likely to be. This negative association isn't surprising granted what we have already seen about the nature of cognitive development. All real learning is active; but television mesmerizes its audience into becoming perfectly passive receptacles for an inexhaustible supply of more or less fascinating images.

That's why school cannot compete with television on its own terms. Television is entertaining because if it isn't, the viewer switches the station. The very survival of a program depends on the instant gratification of its audience. School is just the opposite. Its underlying rationale looks to the future and affirms that hard work and self-discipline in the present will lead to a fuller and more satisfying life later on. The classroom can be an intellectually exciting and lively place, but it takes the active participation of the students to make it so. I'm not issuing a blanket warrant for teachers to be dull or uninspiring in class, but I am taking note of the basic chemistry of intellectual development. Specifically, we should all realize that learning necessarily places serious demands on the student; it requires good-faith effort. School can be exhilarating and fun at times, but it can also be difficult and onerous. For instance, I have yet to meet a professional writer who enjoys writing (as opposed to the distinction of having written). Yet good schools require students to write and rewrite constantly because that's one of the best ways we know to build language mastery and precision of thought. The students suffer through this painful process, but afterwards they feel a sense of genuine accomplishment and increased potency that no TV show could ever give them.

The object lesson for parents is clear. Children can't be expected to understand the long-range benefits of academic discipline, but adults can. At home, it is up to parents to intervene on behalf of the more demanding, but ultimately more rewarding, curriculum. They should make sure that homework comes ahead of television, that children have a quiet place to work, and that they get to bed on time. And they should see that television viewing is kept within reasonable limits—the less, the better.

The gospel of parental involvement is a simple, direct message. Still, if it could only be preached to the already converted, its practical value would be negligible. Happily, our experience in California suggests that the basic message travels well and that increased parental involvement in the schools can serve as a catalyst for dramatic systemwide improvement even in the most difficult circumstances. The Oakland School District is a good example. In the summer of 1984, David Bowick, Oakland's new school superintendent, met with Larry Traumatola, a representative of the Quality Education Project and an experienced community organizer. (The QEP is a nonprofit organization dedicated to helping the schools by arousing public awareness and support. There's more about this group later in this chapter.) The discussion focused on setting concrete, realizable goals that would start Oakland's schools moving in a positive direction from a starting position of low student achievement and low teacher morale.

That summer, QEP set up a series of meetings between Bowick and school faculties at the homes of the principals. Over 2000 teachers voluntarily came to fifty-four meetings and took part in freewheeling discussions. Why had they become involved in education in the first place, they were asked, and how could the Oakland public schools be made more like the system they once dreamed of serving in? The message that Bowick kept hearing was that the lack of parental involvement and support for the work of the schools really hurt.

The district took this message to heart and, with Traumatola providing organizing tips, decided to do something about it. Twenty-five schools were targeted as demonstration sites for building parent support—and they weren't exactly soft touches. In the targeted neighborhoods, 88 to 92 percent of the families had incomes below the poverty level, and more than half were on some form of public assistance. The first goal was to increase the turnout of parents for back-to-school night. Basically, each school ran its parent participation program like a political campaign. In English class, students wrote invitations to their parents asking them to attend. Teachers manned the phones. Contests were held pitting one class against another, with the one having the highest parental attendance rate earning ice cream sundaes.

The strategy worked. From a dismal 15 percent the previous year, attendance at the first back-to-school night in 1985 zoomed to 45 percent. At the meeting, parents heard about the district's goals for improving student achievement and what positive steps they could take at home to help. Obviously, however, with over half the parents absent, there was still plenty of room for improvement. The next goal in the campaign became boosting participation in parent-teacher conferences. This time, phone trees were established. Volunteer parents focused their attention on those parents who hadn't shown up the first time around. The movement began to snowball. Attendance climbed to 65 percent of all parents. To keep open the newly established lines of communication, teachers sent home weekly progress reports with the children's work folders. The parents signed them and wrote back notes. Some came to class as volunteer teacher's aides. By January, enthusiasm for the program had reached such a pitch that Bowick decided to open it up to the rest of the district. The *Oakland Tribune* gave the idea a rousing editorial salute. QEP arranged for seventy school officials to speak from the pulpits of 120 inner city churches on two consecutive Parent Education Sundays. More than 15,000 people heard the message and many in the congregations signed the pledge to spend a half-hour of quiet time a day with their children, to monitor homework, to meet with the teachers, to set a bedtime of no later than 9 P.M. for elementary school children, and so on.

A school system's academic performance doesn't change overnight, of course. But the spirit of community and parental participation in Oakland has infused a new sense of hope there Laverta Henderson, principal of Markham Elementary School, summed up the feeling of her school this way: "It's a whole different thing this year. The more support you receive from parents, the more reward you get from teaching because the kids do better. Last year, no one knew Markham existed. This year, we're on the map and we're on the move!"

Parents don't have to wait for the school district to make the first move, of course. In fact, a small cadre of activist parents who take the trouble to become informed can serve as an effective catalyst for reform progress at the local level. The key to monitoring a school system is to ask the right questions. Parents who have read this book can use it as a primer to identify the vital pressure points.

The obvious jumping-off point for examining school performance is to check the bottom line—academic performance.
At the high school level, what are the average math and verbal
scores of the school's graduating seniors on the SAT or ACT
tests? What has been the trend over the last five years, up or
down? Is the percentage of the class taking the SAT increasing
or decreasing? Similar tests measuring math and reading proficiency exist at the elementary and junior high school levels,
and schoolwide results should be available at the district office
for the asking. (An important reminder: don't be satisfied with
assurance that the school scores equal, or even exceed, the national norms. Students from advantaged backgrounds *ought* to
score above the norm. The real question is how well a school
is doing granted the socioeconomic background of the students
it serves. In California, the hard data for such school-by-school
comparisons is available in annual school performance reports.)

The next area to delve into is the school curriculum. What
are the high school graduation requirements in the district? The
school guidance counselor should have this information. Is the
emphasis on the traditional core of academic subjects—English,
history, mathematics, science, fine arts, and a foreign language?
Is the proportion of students following this academic program
increasing or decreasing? How rigorously are the requirements
defined? To get the answer, talk to the faculty member who is
head of the academic department in which you are interested.
If a student can satisfy the English requirement by taking a
course called Mass Communications, the answer is not rigorously enough. Ask to see a reading list of the short stories and
novels covered in the literature classes. Find out what writing
assignments are given and how often. (Once a week is a bare
minimum for high school students.) For the elementary school

curriculum, checking time allocations for the different subjects is a good way to see if there has been adequate planning. The homeroom teacher should have such a chart worked out and available for review. In a typical 1500-minute week in fourth through sixth grade, for example, California's model time-allocation chart calls for 300 minutes on reading and literature, 200 minutes on "language arts" (spelling, grammar, vocabulary building, writing practice, and so on), 250 minutes on mathematics, 200 on science and health, 200 on history and social studies, 100 on fine arts, 100 on physical education, and 150 minutes of elective time. What is the quality of help for children with special needs—the handicapped, the child attempting to learn English, or the student having problems? Does the school have an effective "safety net" in place?

Next come the questions concerning the rest of the leverage points for reform identified in Chapter Seven: textbooks, discipline, and homework policies. Parents should ask what textbooks are being used in the classroom on a subject-by-subject basis. Are they challenging enough to hold the interest of the students? Or is a seventh-grade class studying a science text written at the fifth-grade reading level? Who is responsible for the decision to use a particular textbook? (The teacher may have been stuck with choosing between the lesser of two evils handed down by the district adopting committee. Find out!) Who has the power to change it? Talk to them. Concerning discipline, a sense of how the school is faring can be picked up by the simple expedient of walking through the place. Are the hallways clear and quiet during classes? Do the students take pride in the appearance of the school? What about a dress code? (Restaurants enforce them, schools can too—and the faculty should take the lead by setting a good example. One of the subtle but effective ways for teachers to establish their authority is by dressing in a neat and professional manner.) Homework is a straightforward proposition. If a teacher rarely assigns homework, a parent should call up and find out why. If a school district or school doesn't have a homework policy, one stating the amount and quality of work students are expected to perform on a daily basis, then it's time to take a look at the people in charge.

As already noted in Chapter Seven, the principal sets the tone for the school. Parents should listen to the principal at back-to-school nights or seek him or her out for a conversation. Is the principal a leader? Does he or she set ambitious goals and have high expectations for the performance of each student? Does he or she know how to get the best out of every teacher and to articulate the school's educational purpose in such a way that the whole community—faculty, students, and parents— coalesces around a guiding vision? How often does the principal monitor the performance of teachers? When was the last time a teacher was terminated or took early retirement? At the district level, the leadership issue becomes one of accountability. If a school is floundering, do the superintendent and board hold the principal accountable for its improvement? How do they go about finding new principals? What are the criteria?

Asking school officials technical questions may make the average parent feel like a pest. It shouldn't. The only way to ascertain the health of a school is by asking the right questions. You would certainly want to know at least as much before buying a new car, and the choice of schools is incomparably more important for your child. If the school officials don't have the answers readily available, that alone tells you something significant. These issues are absolutely central to the educational mission. Competent administrators should have the relevant data at the tips of their fingers. Unfortunately, many "involved" parents never go beyond the superficial level of arguing with a teacher about a child's grades. High grades aren't a meaningful index of school excellence. For example, at the same time a third of California's college-bound seniors were getting mostly A's on their report cards, a performance well above the national average, the state's average SAT scores had fallen far below the national norm.

Parents who take the trouble to find out about their neighborhood schools are doing the system a service, whatever they discover. When the news is good, so much the better. Spread the compliments around. When the school seems deficient in some respect, however, don't just complain. One person who complains is too easily classified as a crackpot. Form a group. When ten or fifteen parents show up at a school board meeting and start focusing on the absence of a homework policy, on the lack of writing assignments, or on the need for principal accountability, they have instant credibility. School boards are very responsive once they understand that there is a constituency for excellence. Because when school boards don't respond, they get replaced—usually by those who raised the reform agenda in the first place.

When I make a public appearance, I can generally count on at least one parent coming up to me and asking the current $64,000 question in education: what about computers? To the best of my knowledge, Aristotle didn't have an Apple IIe in the Athenian Lyceum and quite a lot of learning went on there. Nevertheless, the computer in the classroom has become the modern totem of school progress. Parents whose children attend a school without one fear that they are going to be left behind, and those whose schools have only a few computers want more.

Actually, there's no reason to panic. A computer is a tool, not an end in itself. Children can and will continue to learn without computers because learning takes place in the mind. It is not necessary, or even desirable, for example, that all students learn to program a computer. Thanks to "user-friendly" software, this is a skill most of us will never need to acquire. On the other hand, we *will* find it convenient to use computers increasingly in our day-to-day affairs—to store or retrieve information, to write and edit text, or to do any of a myriad of practical tasks. That fact suggests that the most important reason to have children encounter computers in school is quite simple: to demystify them. We are well on our way to accomplishing that goal. There are already nearly a million computers in daily use in the nation's classrooms.

The computer as a teaching machine is another animal entirely. There are a few things it can do very well, like introducing new math concepts. As a child, I never understood what was occurring in multiplication until I saw my father using his manual adding machine. You could actually watch the columns—the ones, the tens, the hundreds—change position as he cranked it. All of a sudden the concept of multiplication fell into place for me. Good computer programs work the same way. They use color codes and figures to demonstrate visually, on a screen, what the numbers and signs are calling for symbolically. They're great.

Unfortunately, the educational software at more sophisticated levels of instruction has lagged behind the potential of the computer. The real promise of the computer, I believe, lies in the future, with the development of better programs or, more

✳

fancifully, with its wedding to other technologies. I had lunch with George Lucas, the originator of the *Star Wars* saga, at his Lucasfilms studios, and we had a great discussion about how an interactive history course could be set up. The problem with the video format as a teaching tool is that the viewer is made to feel too passive. But through use of the computer, a unit on the Civil War, for example, could be structured so that the student could seek out information in an active fashion. The course Lucas and I talked about would have a set base of video programming with about five times as much material in reserve. When the student asked a key question, this hidden wealth of information would be tapped. Ten- or fifteen-minute reserve segments might show a typical day in the life of a slave, or a profile of Clara Barton, or the battle of the *Merrimac* versus the *Monitor*. The real spellbinders among our teaching staff could be taped talking about the significance of the Dred Scott decision, the beginning of trench warfare, or the New York draft riots. Of course, accomplishing something like this would require a substantial investment in computer-oriented curriculum development. But it would be worth it. We spend over $200 billion a year on education in this country. A relatively small investment of a half of 1 percent of that sum in the fuller use of technology to make sure we were exposing every kindergarten-through-twelfth-grade student to the best materials and teachers available could pay tremendous long-term dividends. I think the U.S. Department of Education is the logical agency to undertake such a school-based Manhattan Project.

The last, but by no means least, important way parents can participate in the excellence movement is by backing it politically. Most of the money for education these days comes from the state legislatures. The special-interest groups realized this early on and organized to claim their share of the pie. By the mid-seventies in California, there were lobbying groups looking out for the interests of bilingual education, of ethnic and women's studies, of the handicapped, learning-impaired, and gifted, of driver's ed and home economics—of just about everything, it seemed, except the school system as a whole. But when we ran a campaign that affirmed the values of a traditional education and tied school reform to adequate funding, it turned out that there was deep support for the schools themselves. Certainly, the hundreds of thousands of letters, telegrams, postcards, and people at rallies made the crucial difference in pushing the reform agenda through the California legislature.

I'm sure the same reservoir of support is available to be tapped in other states. What may be missing, however, is a group like the Quality Education Project to draw it out. The QEP was originally set up to promote the central goals of the reform movement—the core curriculum, homework, high expectations—by eliciting public support for the schools. It was founded by my wife Nancy, along with Tom Ellick, president of the California Manufacturers' Association, noted philanthropist Ann Getty, Randy Knapp, past president and chief executive officer of Wespercorp, Jim Dietz, president of Heald Colleges, and Jeanne Robertson, current president of the QEP. The QEP's basic experience has been that there are hundreds of parents' groups at the school or district level concerned with reform issues. Its job has been to support these groups' efforts.

Toward that end, the QEP has perfected the art of the pro-education rally, a planned gathering of from 1,000 to 10,000 people who come together in support of the public schools. The QEP has compiled a manual that gives a complete organizational structure, job descriptions, and time line for planning such a rally. Videotapes of past rallies are available to demonstrate how to set up the auditorium or stadium and to show the role of the rally director. The QEP also has trained organizers who go into districts and give hands-on management help. In addition, the QEP sponsors retreats and seminars for educators, parents, school board members, and others to discuss pressing education issues, as well as training sessions for parents on the key leverage points for reform. Hopefully, out of this group of activists will come the next generation of school board members, a generation ready to focus the powers of their office on school improvement. If you are interested in the QEP's work or in how to set up a parallel organization in your state, the QEP may be reached at the following address: The Quality Education Project, 2443 Fillmore Street, Suite 101, San Francisco, CA 94115. Fixing our schools will take five to ten years of sustained effort by educators and the resources to do it. To succeed, we are going to need widespread and powerful citizen support to keep quality education high on political agendas.

I began this chapter with the idea that parents are the child's most influential teachers. When one speaks to experienced teachers, however, one quickly hears the opinion voiced that today's students are different. In a report to the President's Commission on Excellence in Education, Herbert Zimales profiled the change in the average child as seen through the eyes of 170 kindergarten-through-twelfth-grade teachers from around the country, each of whom has taught children of middle-class backgrounds for twenty years or longer. The consensus of this group was that today's children grow up more rapidly and are less timid and shy. At the same time, they show much less respect for authority and less self-control, and they take the peer group as a primary reference point for their values and standards much earlier in life. The educators also noted many more instances of personal dishonesty in children: more theft in the schools, more cheating on tests, and a greater readiness to avoid unpleasantness by lying.

Why are these things happening? "Although parents are better educated and tend to value education," Zimales notes in his conclusion, "they are too busy and distracted to take an active interest in their children's schoolwork. They are, for the most part, unwilling or unavailable. . . ." My central theme for parents is that you should be there for your children. They need you, and so do the schools. Together, we have a strong message to impart: that the adult world stands for something coherent and admirable. Only by working together, only through the care and commitment or both parents and teachers, is that message going to get through.

On the other hand, students must face their responsibilities, too. Formal education isn't a burden imposed on them; it's a once-in-a-lifetime opportunity. When you visit schools in Korea or Japan, as I have, the most striking thing you notice is the amount of work that students are willing to do. If it's true that our economy and democracy rest on the quality of education our children receive, then our students are rapidly digging their own graves. When drill instructors train soldiers for battle, they are notoriously hard on them—not out of hate, but because they know what the recruits are going to face. Education is no different. Our students are going to be in deep trouble unless they acquire the skills and knowledge necessary

※

for survival. And we are not doing them any favor by withholding that message.

In the end, the best parents and the best teachers have a lot in common. They love their kids—so much so that they give them the guidance they need to become ethical, socially involved, and productive adults. Indeed, they are prepared to insist on high standards of personal conduct and academic performance. That's the old-fashioned way, and it works when parents and schools practice it together.

CHAPTER TEN

Other Allies: The Universities, the Media, the Feds

THE FATE of the excellence in education movement lies mainly in the hands of those most directly involved: the teachers, the parents, the principals, the administrators, and the students of our 80,000 public elementary and high schools. Still, as John Donne might have put it, "No school is an island, entire of itself." Realistically, reform of the kindergarten-through-twelfth-grade school system is taking place in the context of long-standing institutional arrangements—with the universities, the media, and the federal government—that are themselves in sore need of change. Specifically, the public schools need intellectual leadership from the universities instead of a continuing academic cold shoulder, fresh reporting from the media instead of formula coverage, and deeds to match the encouraging words from the federal government. University professors, reporters and editors, and federal officials all have vital contributions to make to school improvement. In this chapter, we pull back the camera—from a local to a more global perspective—and examine how each of these national institutions (and the individuals who comprise them) can help sustain the momentum for school reform over the long haul.

One of my duties as State Superintendent of Public Instruction is to sit on the Board of Regents of the University of California system and the Board of Trustees of the California State University system. This *ex officio* responsibility recognizes, in theory at least, the close connection between the health of the kindergarten-through-twelfth-grade public school system and the institutions of higher learning. After all, the graduates of the former become the raw recruits of the latter. In fact, the University of California system draws its students from the top 12.5 percent of the state's high school graduates, some of the best and the brightest. During the seventies, however, so many of this select group turned out to write at levels below the minimum acceptable for college work that the University of California system required more than half of them to take Subject A, better known on campus as Bonehead English. But a sizeable number of entrants couldn't even manage that, and so the university was forced to begin offering Pre-Subject A. The college faculties were outraged. What did the public schools mean by sending students to the university so grossly unprepared in the rudiments of academic learning? Apparently, it never occurred to them that in important ways the university was reaping what it had sown.

Let me explain. Basically, the public school system relies on the universities to fulfill two crucial functions: prepare the next generation of teachers and provide intellectual leadership. For example, what do we mean by history? What should be taught in three years of high school history? What people and ideas should be emphasized? How do you best package the material for slow students? for exceptional ones? One problem with U.S. education is that the universities have turned their backs on these plebeian questions and consigned them to the schools

✳

of education. But the schools of education are preoccupied with courses in methodology and technique, often to fulfill state requirements. The net result is that the key business of constantly redefining and improving the academic core has fallen between the cracks.

Teacher education hasn't fared much better. Benton Clark, chairman of the Comparative Higher Education Research Group at UCLA, writes that teacher education in the United States "is a woeful tale of marginality and insecurity—a tale of a large and unkempt Cinderella relegated permanently to a corner. When this pathetic creature is allowed to come to the academic table, she huddles at the far end. The others at the table—representing physics, biology, political science, English, history, and the other disciplines—pretend that she is not there and wish she would go away." The low prestige of the mission is reflected in who ends up doing it. Yale, Harvard, Reed, and Duke all recently dumped their teacher-training programs. According to Clark, the rule of thumb is "the higher the status of the university, the less involvement it is likely to have in teacher education." Education historian Diane Ravitch tells a story that perfectly sums up the prevailing attitudes. She was attending an education symposium at Brown University when a member of the audience volunteered that she had once considered going into teaching but that her faculty advisor had counseled against it. "You're too smart to go into teaching," she had been told.

I find this attitude not just condescending but also remarkably short-sighted. From where does that faculty advisor—or, for that matter, the best universities—suppose the next generation of outstanding students is going to come if not from the classrooms of gifted teachers? It's high time for universities to rethink what they deem worthy of scholarly pursuit. As Coleridge said, there are two kinds of intellectual leadership. There's the avant-garde, tearing down the shibboleths and preparing the way for the new, which is important in a dynamic society. And there's also the lay clerisy, the individuals who are committed to conserving what is best in our tradition and making its basic values come alive for another generation. That's where the public schools need help.

I think university faculties are willing to cooperate in this project if we remove some constraints. I met in Long Beach with representatives of the faculty senate of the California State University system and, in essence, challenged them to get involved. We had a very candid discussion. These were people from the academic disciplines—the sciences, math, history, and so on. Their response was that they were "personally willing," but they also pointed out the facts of university life. Not only were there presently no incentives for a professor to become involved in teacher training or curriculum development, they said, but there were positive penalties. Their peers would look down on such activities. Job performance was judged essentially on the extent and quality of one's original research and scholarship. Survival was still based on the old rule of publish or perish.

I'm not sure how to solve this very different problem but universities must come to grips with it soon. If we are going to attract good people into the profession, teacher training must become as exciting a course of study as any of the traditional academic disciplines. For this to happen, the education theorists and the rest of the faculties have to sit down and reach agreement on how to ensure a well-rounded academic background. I personally favor an arrangement that approximates the European model. There, aspiring secondary school teachers take their degree within the individual discipline they want to teach. Thus, a candidate to teach math majors in mathematics, and so on. In order to guarantee subject mastery, all applicants upon graduation take national examinations testing the depth and breadth of their knowledge. In some countries, less than half pass, and these well-qualified individuals go on to practical training as probationary teachers. This regimen sounds harsh, but it has had a very desirable end result. In Germany or France, teaching in a lycée or gymnasium is considered a respected, even prestigious, occupation.

In the United States, the experience of the rare university educator who bucks prevailing custom and takes an interest in the public schools tends to prove the value of such involvement. Kit Salter, a well-respected professor of geography at UCLA, led the development of a new history/social science curriculum just completed in California. Professor Paul S. Holbo of the University of Oregon history faculty directs workshops for school teachers throughout the western states. Holbo's in-service classes are a blend of readings from contemporary scholarly journals and discussions of new historical interpretations. Once a line of thought has been introduced, Holbo examines how the new material can be presented in class—how taught, how tested, how written about by students. In other words, Holbo's workshops explicitly integrate substantive history with classroom method. He reports that the reaction of his teacher-students has been enthusiastic.

At the risk of exposing myself as a closet anti-intellectual, I would like to make one last comment about the relationship of the universities to the reform movement. Many of the reform steps we have taken in California have had their critics in the schools of education, some of whom have been downright per-

sonally abrasive in their attacks. Our program has been described as "a quick fix," "a political glue sniff," "a garbage can
to toss in every bright idea and private bias that noneducators
had for school improvement," and so on. University-based
critics have argued that our concern with systemwide goals and
results amounts to "top-down" reform, which will never work.
They cite modern management theories—most frequently the
one presented in Thomas Peters's and Robert Watterman's *In
Search of Excellence*—to the effect that innovation springs from
individual initiative and improvement from decentralized authority. In the first place, this is a limited reading. Peters and
Watterman do not advise that enterprises should be completely
decentralized. We tried curricular anarchy in the schools in the
late sixties and early seventies, and it was a disaster. What the
book does say is that a successful corporate enterprise creates a
guiding spirit or vision that informs local effort, legitimizes
standards of excellence, maximizes the autonomy of units to
operate under that vision, and holds everyone accountable for
measurable results. Peters and Watterman call this style "si-
multaneous loose and tight properties," and that's what the
ongoing reform movement is trying to foster.

My main point here, however, is addressed to the skeptics
in the schools of education. Yes, we need constructive criticism
as we move ahead but not personal invective or inflammatory
rhetoric. And what we need even more is practical solutions to
day-to-day problems. Those of us in policy positions are trying
to forge alliances; we're trying to develop a common vision
that everyone can subscribe to and help implement. We need
professors who are willing to roll up their sleeves and enter the
fray. When they take part, they will see how decisions are
reached—in the face of what is politically possible, with im-

*

perfect data to guide us and limited resources to accomplish our ends. (Peters and Watterman, by the way, applaud moving ahead on the basis of prudent hunches and report that companies with "a bias toward action" are more successful.) Too often, some of our university colleagues become paralyzed by the complexities they see in things. As time goes on, of course, we will refine, adjust, and alter our program, as the evidence warrants. But if we had waited for the perfect plan to appear, we would never have started.

The next institution with an important contribution to make to the reform movement is the media. If there's one thing a newspaper reporter can't stand, it's a nonreporter telling him or her how to do the job. Nevertheless, when it comes to the education beat, I think the media—from radio and television to newspapers and magazines—have ample reason for sober self-examination. When I began my campaign, I must have visited every newspaper office in the state making the argument that the schools were not performing and that we needed to re-dedicate them to the principles of a traditional education. Unfortunately, this was two years before the President's Commission on Excellence in Education released its report, "A Nation at Risk," and I found that getting that message across was like screaming into the wind. I would talk for two hours and what would come out was "Bill Honig, former lawyer and political conservative, is running for State Superintendent of Public Instruction." The reporters had been programmed. If you brought up issues of quality, you were a conservative; if you called for more money, you were a liberal. They didn't know what to do with someone who argued for both.

My point is that an evil prince didn't kiss the public school system on the blackboard one morning in the seventies and turn it into a toad. The decline in quality took place over a period of many years during which school officials, who should have known better, basically failed to stick to their knitting. Reporters are the all-purpose watchdogs of our society. If a judge has an unusual number of cases overturned on appeal or if a surgical procedure such as the coronary by-pass turns out not to prolong the lives of the patients who undergo it, we expect to read about it in the popular press. My question is, where was the in-depth coverage when the public school system was going downhill?

The answer is that too many education reporters were sitting in the audience at school board meetings, pencils poised, preparing to write about the latest collective bargaining session with the teachers' union, the proposed centralization of the school lunch program, or if they were especially enterprising, the internecine wrangling over the superintendent's travel allowance. The last thing on their minds was how well the schools were doing the job of educating the kids.

That's too bad. Good education reportage at the local level requires getting out of the district office and into the schools to identify patterns of success and failure. A sharp reporter on the education beat is likely to ask many of the same questions an interested parent might: How well are the schools performing? Are the indices headed up or down? Who is responsible and what are they doing about it? The best education reporters in California, people like David Savage of the *Los Angeles Times* or Richard Colvin of the *Oakland Tribune,* write stories that reflect on the basic purpose of the schools. These reporters have a knack for finding the local story and using it to illustrate the broader issues. I can't say I always like what they turn up in their digging around. But it's better to be embarrassed by a problem and have to correct it than to be ignorant about its existence and do nothing.

At this stage, probably the biggest danger for the media is the temptation to continue covering the last war. In the fall of 1984—a year and a half after the President's Commission issued its warning—the ABC network aired a special report, "To Save Our Schools, To Save Our Children." It was three hours of unrelieved gloom and doom. It showed white flight from inner city schools, an incompetent teacher overwhelmed by a classroom full of rowdy kids, and a gifted teacher in Los Angeles deciding to quit because of the lousy pay. I called up Marshall Frady, who wrote and narrated the program, and chided him for its one-sided slant. A lot was going on to turn things around, a lot that he could have included, I pointed out. It's fine to show the problem, but you should also let people know what they can do about it. You don't just leave them hanging there with a feeling of despair. I must have sounded like a typical thin-skinned bureaucratic Pollyanna to him. So be it. But I learned in my campaign that you don't exist until the media says you do. The public wasn't aware of the decline of the schools until years after it began. The reform movement is what's happening today; it's a grass-roots phenomenon; it's real and it's newsworthy. In my opinion, the press should be giving it more extensive coverage.

The final institution with tremendous power to help keep the excellence movement on track is the federal government. On the bright side, the new secretary of the Department of Education, Bill Bennett, is thoroughly committed to the excellence movement. As chairman of the National Endowment for the Humanities, he worked tirelessly to restore the vitality of the humanities curriculum in U.S. higher education and currently is using the visibility of his office to campaign for a curriculum of substance. And President Reagan has also used the "bully pulpit" of his office to stump for a resurgence of the public schools.

However, the truth is that the federal government has been reluctant to follow with financial support. This became evident at an education forum at Pioneer High School in Whittier, California, where Reagan keynoted the morning session. I was in the audience and I remember the anticipation in the crowd that day, the arrival of the Presidential entourage by helicopter, and the burst of pride in the room as the band struck up "Hail to the Chief." It was an impressive event. But once all the hoopla was over and the press had left, the educators remained behind with quizzical looks on their faces. Now what? I was on the panel for the afternoon session and my message to them was simple. "Look," I said, "we should absolutely thank our lucky stars that the President is pushing hard for the philosophy we have been talking about—standards, expectations, a core curriculum. That's terrific. But to come in and say that we want excellence in education but we're not willing to pay a fair share shows that they are not really serious."

There's no doubt that President Reagan is right when he says that education is primarily a state responsibility. The budget figures back him up on that. In California, for example, only 7 percent of the public school funds derive from the federal government. Nevertheless, these monies can make a huge difference in some of the developmental and equity areas in which the federal government has pioneered. If the refrom movement is to retain its credibility, we cannot afford to turn our back on any segment of our youth. And that's why I have testified in congressional hearings against the cutbacks in recent federal education budgets.

Take the Reagan administration's proposal for fiscal year 1986, for example. The most important commitment the nation has made in education over the past fifteen years has been to expand the opportunities of our "at-risk" children: the handicapped, the disadvantaged, and the non–English speaking. Several major programs have been launched in the last decade and have achieved generally favorable results. In the budget for fiscal year 1986, however, a cut of $338 million in education aid to immigrants, for nutrition, and so on was proposed. If this was just part of a general belt-tightening, that would be one thing. But, in the same budget, a $350 million income tax credit was proposed for parents of children attending private schools. In effect, $350 million in resources was shifted out of the public schools, which serve 88 percent of the nation's youth, and into the private schools, which generally cater to a more economically privileged group.

I'm not opposed to helping the private schools, but I think it should be done in a more equitable fashion. It would be far preferable, I believe, for the federal government to spend its education dollars on research and development that would benefit all students. We need help with widespread in-service training of the present corps of teachers if we are going to be successful in bringing to life the ambitious curriculum proposed. The federal government started to do this in the math and science fields in 1984 with a limited program, but the same need exists for English and history and the rest of the academic courses. In a similar vein, no one really knows how to train effective principals, even though the evidence suggests that a good principal is the key player in successful schools. The federal government should address this problem by setting up institutes to help groom our future school leaders.

With its highly leveraged research grants to induce universities to cooperate, the U.S. government could also make a huge difference in the area of curriculum development. There is ample precedent. The National Science Foundation has funded curriculum development in the natural sciences ever since the Russians sent up *Sputnik*. Today, well over half the school districts in the United States use one or more of the federally funded science programs in the seventh through twelfth grades. Back in the early fifties, the complaint about the standard science fare was that it stressed rote memorization at the expense of acquiring a sense of the dynamic of inquiry and of the scientific method in practice. Since then, the NSF science programs have greatly improved the content and approach of science teachers in return for a relatively modest investment. It worked in science, and I believe federal funding can help with curriculum development in the other academic disciplines as well. We need to develop the core curriculum in a variety of forms for children at different learning levels and from different backgrounds. They will all take history and literature, of course, and they will also all learn about freedom, the structure of government, and the moral and ethical principles around which our society coheres. But the stories that get these points across will vary. There's a great deal of work to be done in this area. The objection, I know, is that such a program will eventually lead to a single national curriculum. The truth is, however, that we already have such a curriculum, only it is being written by textbook publishers at a regrettably diminished level. It would

✳

be far better, I believe, to have the government spend some seed money to help flesh out an elementary and secondary humanities curriculum that had some real substance to it. After this goal has been reached, then the fruits of these labors should be shared on an equitable basis with the private schools. In this way, we improve the education of all our children, without pitting the welfare of one group against the interests of the other.

The federal government's basic commitment to the equity agenda needs to be reaffirmed but that doesn't mean these programs can't be improved. Right now they are overadministered and overregulated. For instance, the government sends about $70 million a year in federal monies to California so that we can deliver special education service to migrant children. But, we estimate, by the time the various bureaucrats along the way have taken their bites of the apple, only one-half to one-third of the total dollars appropriated actually reach the classrooms where the kids are.

Some programs are simply poorly designed. The federal Chapter I program for disadvantaged students, for instance, was drawn up so that you could only use its monies to aid children who scored below the fiftieth percentile on skills tests. This is ridiculous on several counts. First, the greater the number of students who move above the norm under this program, the less money a school receives—so there is a built-in incentive not to succeed. Second, it takes a small army of accountants to administer the program. And, third, why define disadvantaged in terms of educational level, anyway? The idea is to help all kids from low-income neighborhoods get a good start in life, not just the educational underachievers. The unfortunate consequence of the federal Chapter I definition of disadvantaged was to set up schools-within-schools in which, paradoxically, you could only get special attention if you did poorly.

In California, we tried something different. We arranged an experiment with five elementary schools in poor black neighborhoods in Oakland. Rather than aiming an aid package at a segment of their students, however, we gave the schools money to upgrade the quality of instruction and staff across the board. Some very interesting things began to happen. The average kids, who had been getting absolutely short-changed under the older Chapter I definition, put on the academic afterburners and went into orbit. On reading and math tests, they were typically making fifteen-months progress in a school year. Meanwhile, the below-average kids showed more progress in this environment than they had when the remedial programs were targeted exclusively at them. These results provide a basic insight into education reform. In our desire to save the slow learners, we have been throwing out life preservers, one after another. But the best way to help the floundering learner (and everyone else) is to make sure that the lifeboat itself—the school—is seaworthy.

The feds, in other words, should design their equity programs to strengthen the school unit, That means respecting the autonomy and creativity of the on-site personnel. I have already talked about the concept of bureaucratic self-restraint at the state and district levels. It would behoove the U.S. Department of Education to exercise a little of the same discipline. Is the federal goal that disadvantaged kids do better? Fine—get the money in the hands of the low income districts and schools as expeditiously as possible. Build in incentives for success. Then hold local officials accountable for results. We don't need a set

✳

of "guidelines" as thick as a telephone book written by lawyers for the benefit of accountants. We need the money to be put where it counts—where the kids are.

In fact, the theme of this chapter might well be the need to focus on results. As the universities, media, and federal government do so, they will better discharge their unique responsibilities, and the school reform movement will be that much stronger for its new allies.

CHAPTER ELEVEN

Passing On the Flame

ONE OF THE warmest surprises of the recent Los Angeles Olympic Games was the reception accorded the Olympic torch as it traveled across the heartland of this country. From dawn to dusk, quiet knots of citizens—housewives, farmers, teenagers, and retirees—assembled along our back roads and byways to watch a white-clad figure run by with the flame from Mt. Olympus held proudly aloft. No one told these citizens that they should come out and witness this passage, but they did—by themselves or with a companion, in the tens, and thousands, and finally millions—to pay tribute to the ideals of good sportsmanship, friendly competition, the striving for excellence, and peace on earth among nations. Surprised reporters didn't know quite what to make of this spontaneous outpouring. They wrote about the resurgence of a "new patriotism." But, I think the explanation was far more deeply rooted in human nature.

We are all looking for meaning in our lives. And, when a symbol comes along that powerfully expresses our collective hope for a better world, we embrace it. Unfortunately, we are so often numbed by the evidence of the evil of which humanity is capable that we tend to lose sight of an equally formidable capacity for good. But, even when we forget it, that great reservoir of good will in society remains available to be tapped.

About the same time the Olympic torch was making its triumphant cross-country journey, we were holding a series of rallies in support of quality education in California. These were almost old-fashioned Chautauqua meetings in tone, with balloons and flags and stem-winding speeches and a rousing rendition of "America the Beuatiful" as parents signed their pledges of support for their children and schools. Reporters had the same pinch-me-I-must-be-dreaming reaction to all this. In San Luis Obispo, for instance, a veteran of World War II was standing in the crowd with tears flowing down his cheeks. A skeptical reporter walked up to him and asked what was the matter. This was a hard-bitten fellow but he didn't flinch. "I haven't had feelings like this since I was in uniform," he answered. "I realized something for the first time tonight. It's just not American to be against the public schools."

I think that's exactly right, not in the negative way Senator Joe McCarthy once used the term, but in an affirmative, descriptive sense. For what is more fundamental to our national temperament than a buoyant optimism about the future? From the beginning, the premise of universal education has always been the hope for a better tomorrow. Three centuries ago, Timothy Dwight of Connecticut put it this way in a homely, colonial-era quatrain:

> *How bless'd this heavy distinguished land,*
> *Where schools in every hamlet stand;*
> *Far spread the beams of learning bright,*
> *And every child enjoys the light. . . .*

✳

From Benjamin Franklin to Walter Lippmann, faith in education has been one of the recurring chords in the American tone poem. It is part of our national identity, and the public school system is its concrete expression. The hallowed status of education, however, does not confer on it indefinite immunity to change. Education is much too important to the maintenance of this democracy to allow the public schools to fail. If the present system can't be made to work, then we will have to find one that can.

Critics are becoming increasingly impatient. After the President's Commission filed its report, Peter Brimelow argued in *Fortune* that the excellence movement stood little chance of success because reform didn't serve the interests of the educational bureaucracies. "The public school system is the American version of Soviet agriculture," he declared, "beyond help as currently organized because its incentive structure is all wrong." The cure for the problems of a socialized monopoly, he prescribed, was a "good dose of competition" in the form of a voucher system. (A voucher system would provide parents with an annual voucher worth whatever the school district was spending per pupil. The parents could use it to send their child to any accredited school of their choice.) Theoretically, the market discipline thus imposed would encourage more diversity in the kinds of schools available and more efficiency in the way they were run. As schools competed against one another to attract more students (and dollars), survival of the fittest would guarantee superior quality.

Such a sweeping proposal has a certain revolutionary appeal to it, to be sure, but I would hoist a couple of warning flags. From a strictly pragmatic point of view, scrapping the present system on the off chance that the array of free-lance efforts drummed up to replace it would be better performers is fairly risky. I have been involved in the start-up of a new school, Second Community in San Francisco, and, believe me, it doesn't just happen. Even among people with the best of intentions, there are arguments, misunderstandings, conflicts of purpose, and fallings out. To extend the free-enterprise analogy Brimelow introduced, founding a new school is somewhat like starting a small business. The majority don't make it past the first couple of years. The difference is that, if your great idea for franchising creamed beets with orange sauce doesn't turn a profit, you take a financial bath and go on to the next great idea; but when a new school fails academically, the lasting victims are the children cheated of a chance to learn. That's a good reason to tread lightly.

An even better one becomes apparent when you consider what else we stand to lose with a voucher system—namely, the village square. In a culture that celebrates the prerogatives of the individual, the public schools are potentially one of the most meaningful forces for social cohesion. They are uniquely situated to serve as a forum for identifying common values and aspirations. Indeed, the work that sets them apart from the private schools may very well be the providing of a place where all our children can come together and discover what it is that binds us as a people. A voucher system gives up on achieving such a consensus. It says, to each his own. The net result would be one less unifying force in a society wholly dependent on the voluntary allegiance of individuals for survival.

I find it ironic that because the public schools are public, some critics believe they cannot stand for any normative values—for example, constancy over infidelity, or magnanimity over self-absorption, or industry over laziness—but instead must ever wear the institutional poker face of moral neutrality. In my opinion, just the opposite conclusion makes more sense. Because public school are public, they *must* take part in those crucial discussions that vitally concern the community, that cry out for adult guidance. The shared ethos of our diverse and pluralistic society is preeminently the subject of the public schools.

Despite what his fundamentalist critics wrote about him, Charles Darwin did not believe that his theory of evolution showed that humans dwelt on the same spiritual plain as the apes or nature's other fauna. The important distinction, he wrote, was the existence of conscience—"the feeling of the individual that he belongs to a group, and owes it some measure of loyalty and consideration." "Morality," Darwin went on, "is the co-operation of the part with the whole, and of each group with some larger whole. Civilization would be impossible without it." Civilization, morality, cooperation, conscience—the words may vary, but the role of the public schools remains the same, to build a sense of belonging and responsibility to the community in its students. That doesn't mean that each public school must be a clone of the next one or that there is no room for choice or innovation. Indeed, the magnet school movement—the establishment of special-theme academies in the performing arts, sciences, and humanities—is one of the most exciting new programs in public education.

Sometimes, we concentrate on the imperfections of our school system so intently that we lose sight of the magnitude of what we have undertaken. The U.S. education system remains unmatched in its ambition. Year in and year out, three-quarters of our eighteen-year-olds graduate from high school. In western Europe, fewer than half the adolescents, 36 percent, stay in school that long. And in Great Britain, only 17 percent continue their studies to that age. We take the notion of universal education for granted, but it didn't have to be that way. Ben Jonson ridiculed the idea. "A little learning to a poor man is a dangerous thing," he counseled, ". . . those who are born to poverty and drudgery should not be deprived by an improper education of the opiate of ignorance." Now that the excellence movement is asserting itself, the great-great-great-grandchild of this opinion is making itself felt once again. The thesis is that excellence is incompatible with mass education because, as education professor Mary Woodworth Watrous wrote in the *Wall Street Journal,* some children just don't have the mental capacity. "It is hard to tell a parent that Johnny can't understand algebra because he just isn't smart enough," she wrote, "but Johnny knows it, and so does the teacher, even if the chaps on the National Commission on Excellence in Education . . . don't." Watrous recommended the European pattern as more practical. "The [various commissions] would serve the nation better if they stopped dreaming about this kind of excellence for all and instead instructed the American public in the realities of education," she concluded.

Watrous and others are concerned that the schools will be unable to deliver on the promise of a rigorous education for all students and that we are setting them up for failure. That may be, but I think it's a risk worth taking for several reasons. First of all, no one in the excellence movement is saying that all students must reach the same pinnacle of erudition. Obviously, there are differences in aptitude and intelligence that must be reflected in the scope and pace of the curriculum. What we do affirm, however, is that the great majority of our high school students, the middle 50 percent now whiling away their time in the catch-as-catch-can general track, are not working up to their potential. They are not being challenged. And that can't continue.

To sit back and conduct business as usual when we know we are providing students with less than they need is unconscionable. Critics like Watrous shouldn't be so eager to find excuses for nonperformance because the fact is that too many perfectly capable students end up taking the easy way out and paying a terrible price for it later on. We should be as worried about losing students' attention by undertaxing them as we are about asking too much of them. Indeed, my philosophy is closer to Robert Browning's: "Ah, but a man's reach should exceed his grasp, or what's a heaven for?" Every student can't master the intricacies of calculus and there's no shame in that. But every student can do his or her best. And because we love them, we owe our children at least that much—to demand that they make an honest effort.

Taking a chance on excellence is risky, but the risk of doing nothing—and losing the public schools—threatens the very fabric of our democracy. The public schools have long been the backbone of our democracy, not just because they train citizens but because of what they say about individual worth and opportunity. In the United States, the unspoken promise has always been that it's what you can do, not whose child you are, that matters. Thomas Jefferson insisted on this point. Exceptional talent was distributed randomly through the population, he wrote, independent of wealth or social status, and the only way to ensure that the "natural aristocrats" among us contributed their full measure to the new nation was to provide schooling for every child. One need look no further than a list of our Presidents, many of whom were of humble origins, like Lincoln, Truman, or Ronald Reagan himself, to appreciate the accuracy of Jefferson's prophecy. Thanks to the public schools, social mobility, both up and down the scale, is a fact of life in the United States to a far greater degree than in the rest of the world. I would hate for our generation to be the one that lost its nerve, forgot its roots, and presided over the demise of an education system that historically has served us so well.

I am optimistic that we can avoid such a decline. Public, political, business, and minority leaders are all demanding excellence, and I think the schools are capable of delivering it. The work is underway nationwide. In Texas, the legislature passed the first general tax increase since 1971 to finance generous salary increases and a new career ladder for teachers: the first statewide prekindergarten instruction program for children of the poor was set up, and strict academic standards were established for all student athletes. In Florida, school districts now get more money to keep class sizes down if they require at least 5000 words of writing per semester from each high school student. Kentucky has approved "forgiveness loans" for college students majoring in science and mathematics who agree to teach for three years in the state's public schools. Clearly, the lawmakers are backing the excellence agenda with hard cash, but there's even more good news. In December of 1984, the U.S. Department of Education released a rating of the states on such key academic indicators as dropout rates and SAT scores. Such a "report card" would have been stridently resisted a few years ago; today, the idea of setting goals and living up to them is accepted as a proper national concern.

The momentum is building and the base of support is broadening. The National Commission on Secondary Schooling for Hispanics came out in early 1985 in favor of a core curriculum for all students. Hispanic students were too often shunted into the vocational or general track, the commission reported. In California, we have received tremendous support from the business community. The Los Angeles Education Partnership, for example, is supported by several major corporations (including Atlantic-Richfield, TRW, and Lockheed). LAEP awarded 250 grants to teachers in 1985 to pay for special classroom projects of their own invention. In Silicon Valley, Apple, IBM, Hewlett-Packard, and other companies have provided more than $900,000 in support to local school districts including a special computer education program that runs from kindergarten to classes for senior citizens. All in all, the situation in California is promising. We have our financial incentives in place for teachers; our academic curriculum is shaping up; the accountability program has gotten underway, and the first results exceed our target; writing and homework are on the increase; test scores have begun to rise; school leaders know what's expected of them. Our schools are poised for a great leap forward—but nothing is guaranteed.

Nothing is guaranteed because, ultimately, turning around the schools depends on the good will and cooperation of countless individuals. If the various interest groups and lobbies decide to find fault and assign blame in every phase of the undertaking but their own, nothing will change. I know that teachers, in particular, are tired and mistrustful from the roller-coaster ride of the past decades. As Diane Ravitch has pointed out, a teacher whose career began in 1960 has lived through an "era of failed revolutions." These include the teaching machine movement, the open education movement, the free school movement, the deschooling movement, the minimum competency movement, the back to basics movement, to name a few. "The veteran teacher may be excused for secretly thinking, 'this too shall pass.' " Ravitch writes.

That much having been said, however, it is also worth noting that substantial differences exist this time around. For the first time in a generation, concern for the state of the public schools has rekindled the public imagination. Activist groups plumping for novel ideals like open education or values clarification relied on a small but passionate base of support. In comparison, the excellence movement already qualifies as a proven grass-roots strategy for political organizing. Its common-sense recommendations in favor of homework, more writing, a core academic curriculum, classroom discipline, and high expectations enjoy broad public support and are the quickest route to that other vital component of school improvement—adequate funding. Parents, teachers, students, and administrators have a huge job ahead of them, no doubt; but by working together on a cause that makes sense to the mainstream of the society, they can prevail. For this to happen, however, all of us have to open our eyes and agree to some self-evident truths: that cooperation is better than recrimination; that school reform is a long-term process, not a once-in-a-lifetime event; and that the schools won't ever be made to function perfectly, but they can be made to function better tomorrow than they do today, and better yet on the day after that.

I think the field of education is the most exciting place to be in our society right now. The echo of the baby boom is already on the way, and we'll have to be resourceful in how we cope with the increased number of students. More buildings will be required but that isn't the answer by itself. It makes sense first to stretch our resources by using the buildings we already have more efficiently, by going to a schedule of rotating quarters with a summer session in some schools. Summer vacation was originally an accommodation to a farm economy; the children were needed to bring in the harvest. Later, with the popularity of the large family, people resisted changing because the summer vacation was the only chance to travel together as a family. Now, however, the average family size is much smaller, and a pressing reason to use buildings year round is at hand. To cope with the growing incidence of latchkey kids, we should start offering after-school activities, in sports, the arts, and foreign languages, to make good use of the hours between the final bell and when mom or dad comes home. When I was superintendent at Reed, we tried such a self-financing program in conjunction with the local parks department, and it was a popular success. We need to explore giving parents more choice and alternatives in where they can send their child to school and what kind of programs are available. Magnet schools have proven particularly effective. We shouldn't be afraid to innovate, but we should never innovate at the expense of our basic education mission.

To be an educator today is to be like one of the citizens of Athens addressed in Pericles funeral oration. In that stirring speech, individuals are called upon to imagine the spectacle of the great city before them and in their admiration to remember that "all this greatness she owes to men with the fighter's daring, the wise man's understanding of his duty, and the good man's self-discipline in its performance. . . ." In short, to be an educator today is to be called to action.

We have a long way to go, it's true; but the encouraging thing is that we've already come a long way from the dreary days when the schools were floundering and no one seemed to notice or care. Does everyone remember the tag end of the sixties? Back then in San Francisco, if you happened to pick up a hitchhiker, you'd hear that the revolution was happening to-morrow. Word came back that a good friend strung out on drugs had killed himself in the mountains of Columbia, and no one said anything about it. I remember riding a bicycle through Golden Gate Park and encountering a typical period scene with Hare Krishnas in one corner, street people here and there, a meditation circle looking for its center—every variety of ex-hibitionist vying for attention. A sense of how atomized and fragmented our society was becoming struck me. I went home and wrote down my thoughts. My sense was that my genera-tion was refusing to grow up: we were abdicating our respon-sibility to stand for something. To all outward appearances, we had the trappings of adulthood—jobs, marriages, dependents—but emotionally we were still children in the park. That's when I decided that the world could probably survive with one less lawyer but that one more teacher might make a difference.

I've never regretted that decision. I think the center of our culture is reasserting itself, not least of all by reclaiming the public schools as a vehicle for transmitting our core beliefs. Like the runner bearing the Olympic torch aloft, each genera-tion is the keeper of the flame—the distilled wisdom and values of our civilization's collective past—and is duty-bound to pass this heritage on. If you believe, as I do, that our form of gov-ernment and the Enlightenment principles on which our coun-try was founded represent the best hope for this world, then the precious nature of this trust is evident. I have no doubt that we will be equal to the task.

The excellence movement will succeed because it must suc-ceed—for our future, for our children. It has already legitimized

✳

the efforts of a corps of the best teachers, administrators, and parents. And where this corps leads, others will follow. If this book has made any point, it should be that there is plenty of work for everyone to do. The key question is this: will enough individuals take responsibility for doing it? Will enough individuals have the courage to start with their particular classroom, their particular school, and their particular school district and work to make each a little better?

It is largely an anonymous, thankless task. Who will notice the history teacher who corrects papers not just for content but for writing style? Who will commend the principal who supports such dedication and makes each teacher feel part of a larger, sensible, effort? Who will thank parents for turning off the television and spending time finding out about their child's hopes and dreams? And yet, the cumulative effect of these little victories is the stuff of which excellence is made. The school reform movement has little to offer those who take part in it but hard work, long hours, and the distant promise of a society worthy of our highest ideals. Let's get to it!

Jobs and Education

THE CORRELATION between education and earning power has been amply documented over the years. The general rule is that the higher the level of academic attainment a given individual achieves, the more money he or she is likely to command in the marketplace. But what about the macroeconomic picture? Does society really need to train the majority of youngsters to high levels of academic excellence? A consensus of educators has long answered that question in the affirmative. Recent studies by the National Academy of Science ("High School and the Changing Workplace," Washington, D.C., 1984) and by the College Board ("Academic Preparation for Work," New York, July 1984) reach remarkably consistent conclusions. Specifically, both groups found that our economy is heading in the direction of requiring higher skill levels in employees and that job opportunities in the future will favor the well educated.

Recently, however, a pair of researchers affiliated with the Stanford University School of Education, Russell Rumberger and Henry Levin, released a report coming to the opposite conclusion. The document (Project Report No. 84-A4 of the

Institute for Research on Education Finance and Governance) focused on Bureau of Labor Statistics projections of future employment in the United States. It argues that future job growth will be greater in service and clerical jobs that require little or no postsecondary schooling and that pay below-average wages. This analysis, undercutting as it did one of the fundamental rationales for the academic curriculum, caused quite a bit of soul-searching in academic circles. I would like to review in this appendix the important issues that Rumberger and Levin's report raises and suggest an alternative interpretation of the BLS forecast.

Rumberger and Levin's argument, in essence, is that the impact of high-technology industries and occupations has been oversold. They correctly point out that, even when broadly defined high-tech industries employ only 15 percent of the work force. Although they concede that the highest rate of job growth in the economy will be in the glamorous high-tech occupations, they contend that the largest absolute growth will continue to occur in the familiar, lunch-bucket, low-education occupations. To buttress this point, they present in Table 4 of their report a list of the ten fastest-growing job categories, both relatively and absolutely, based on BLS projections through the year 1995. The table shows that the fastest relative growth is predicted to occur in job categories such as computer systems analyst, legal assistant, electrical engineer, and so on. But the largest absolute growth will be in categories such as building custodian, cashier, secretary, and truck driver. The message from the BLS figures is clear, according to Rumberger and Levin. "Not only will high tech provide few job opportunities in the future economy," they write, "but most new jobs will require no postsecondary schooling and will pay wages significantly lower than the average."

Rumberger and Levin's table is misleading for two reasons. In the first place, the chart is biased toward the broadest job classifications. For instance, the job of custodian, which makes the top ten list for most openings, is a catchall. The BLS breaks down the job category of engineering much more discretely. If one adds up the jobs in all the engineering categories in the BLS forecast, one finds that there will be 420,000 new (education-requiring) jobs in this field by 1995, which puts engineering in the top ten range. In the second place, one can't just look at new jobs to evaluate the education required of today's students. Total job openings are made up of both newly created jobs and net replacements. Even slow-growing categories require large numbers of replacements. To take an example out of my own area of expertise, secondary school teachers don't show up in Rumberger and Levin's table since this category will grow by only about 100,000 new jobs by 1995. But since there are currently a million secondary school teachers, there will be an additional 500,000 openings in this field by 1995, assuming a typical annual retirement and attrition rate of 4 percent.

A better way to read the BLS projections is to look at the aggregate data and see what they say. Using 1982 as the base year, the BLS reports that 101 million people were working. By broad categories, there were 16.6 million professional, 9.5 million managerial, 7 million sales, 19 million clerical, 11.5 million craft, 16.2 million service, 13 million operative, 5.9 million laborer, and 2.7 million farm. Based on my reading of Department of Labor job categories, 38 percent of the 1982 work force had high levels of education and training (see Table A). Between 1982 and 1995, according to the BLS, 58.6 million job openings (including new jobs and net replacements) are projected to become available (see Table B). Of these (using the same assumptions as for Table A), 27.1 million, or 46 percent of the total, are expected to require higher levels of academic preparation. In other words, broadly interpreted, we are moving from a work force in which 38 percent have the computation, speaking, writing, and thinking skills associated with the college bound, to a labor market in which nearly half the new hires will be expected to be so qualified. That's a significant trend—and a clear indicator to the public schools. Making allowances for possible underprojections and for maximizing the opportunities for our young people, my conclusion from the BLS projections is that we should be attempting to educate at least two-thirds to three-quarters of our students to these higher levels of academic achievement.

Interestingly enough, predicting a low-skills employment fu-

TABLE A: U.S. JOBS, 1982

	TOTAL	HIGH-LEVEL EDUCATION	LOW-LEVEL EDUCATION
Professional	16.6	16.6	—
Managerial	9.5	9.5	—
Sales	7.0	2.0	5.0
Clerical	19.0	3.8	15.2
Craft	11.5	3.5	8.0
Service	16.2	1.5	14.7
Operative	13.0	—	13.0
Laborer	5.9	—	5.9
Farm	2.7	1.5	1.2
Total	101.4	38.4	63.0
	(100%)	(38%)	(62%)

✳

TABLE B: PROFILE OF JOB OPENINGS, 1982–1995

	HIGH-LEVEL EDUCATION		LOW-LEVEL EDUCATION	
	New	Replacement	New	Replacement
Professional	5.2	6.6	—	—
Managerial	2.7	4.5	—	—
Sales	0.6	0.7	1.4	1.3
Clerical	2.0	1.1	3.0	4.4
Craft	1.1	1.3	2.0	2.1
Service	0.4	0.4	4.1	3.6
Operative	—	—	1.1	4.0
Laborer	—	—	2.4	1.8
Farm	(0.1)	0.6	(0.1)	0.4
Subtotal	11.9	15.2	13.9	17.6

Total High-Level Education	27.1	(46%)
Total Low-Level Education	31.5	(54%)
Total Job Openings	58.6	(100%)

ture, as Rumberger and Levin do, merely updates a social prophecy originally made by Karl Marx—that the capitalist system would inexorably force more and more workers into low-paying jobs or out on the streets, setting the stage for a proletarian revolution. Marx was wrong, as the growth of the huge middle class in the United States and western Europe attests. He failed to anticipate the genius of the free market system in adapting to technological change by reinvesting the wealth it helped create in new products and services, thus generating more jobs and continuing the upward spiral of economic prosperity.

From the loom-smashing Luddites of eighteenth-century England to the present, every time a technological innovation that threatened to change business as usual was introduced, there have been people who foresaw imminent disaster. And history shows that every time they have been proven wrong. But in the most remarkable statement of their treatise, Rumberger and Levin suggest that this time "history may tell us very little about the future." Why so? The industrial and agricultural revolutions only replaced muscle power, but future technologies "could greatly reduce the mental demands of work in virtually all sectors of the economy."

Maybe, but I sincerely doubt it. Anyone who has ever worked with computers knows that the machines are idiots savants. They are unparalleled at performing their limited tasks but totally incapable of the judgments and creative intelligence that make human employees valuable. And the experience of businesses that extensively rely on computers seems to be bearing this point of view out. In March of 1985, Adia Personnel Services of Menlo Park, California, conducted a survey of almost 1000 companies in eight countries, asking what effect office automation had had on their staffing. The answer: "Although the total number of jobs did not change, many lower-level office workers were laid off and replaced by more skilled personnel." A recent report by a major insurance company examined the reading level of the material that a variety of their employees— secretaries, clerks, typists—were expected to comprehend. It turned out that the expectations were quite high.

The conclusion is inescapable. To bet on a low-tech future would be foolish, unfair to our children, and dangerous to the economic health of this country.

*

Bibliography

Adelson, Joseph. "How the Schools Were Ruined." *Commentary*, July 1983.
Adler, Mortimer J. *The Paodeia Proposal: An Educational Manifesto.* New York: Macmillan, 1982.
———. *Paodeia Problems and Possibilities.* New York: Macmillan, 1983.
———. *The Paodeia Program: An Educational Syllabus.* New York: Macmillan, 1984.
Anderson, Richard, C. "Reading Research and Reading Practice." In *Computers in Education: Realizing the Potential.* Report of a Research Conference, Pittsburgh, PA. November 1982. Washington, DC: US Government Printing Office, 1983.
Bell, Daniel. *The Cultural Contradictions of Capitalism.* New York: Basic Books, 1976.
Bellah, Robert N., Richard T. Madsen, William M. Sullivan, Ann Swidler, and Steven M. Tipton. *Habits of the Heart.* University of California Press, 1985.
Bennett, William J. "'To Reclaim a Legacy': Text of Report on Humanities in Education." *The Chronicle of Higher Education.* November 28, 1984.
Boyer, Ernest L. *High School: A Report on Secondary Education in America.* The Carnegie Foundation for the Advancement of Teaching. New York: Harper & Row, 1983.
Bunzel, John H., Ed. *Challenge to American Schools.* New York: Oxford University Press, 1985.
Chall, Jeanne S. *Learning to Read: The Great Debate.* New York: McGraw-Hill, 1983.

Clark, Burton R. "The High School and the University: What Went Wrong in America." *Phi Delta Kappan,* February and March 1985.

Commager, Henry Steele. *The Commonwealth of Learning.* New York: Harper & Row, 1968.

Dewey, John. *Experience and Education.* Kappa Delta Pi Lecture Series. New York: Macmillan, 1938.

Finn, Chester E., Jr., Diane Ravitch, and Robert T. Fancher, Eds. *Against Mediocrity: The Humanities in America's High Schools.* New York: Holmes & Meier, 1984.

Finn, Chester E., Jr., Diane Ravitch, and P. Holley Roberts, Eds. *Challenge to the Humanities.* New York: Holmes & Meier, 1984.

Finn, Chester E., Jr. " 'Gee, Officer Krupke' and Other Barriers to Excellence in the Schoolroom." *Policy Review,* Summer 1984.

———. "The Excellence Backlash: Sources of Resistance to Educational Reform." *The American Spectator,* September 1984.

———. "Teacher Politics." *Commentary,* February 1983.

———. "Toward Strategic Independence: Nine Commandments for Enhancing School Effectiveness." *Phi Delta Kappan,* April 1984.

Gaff, Jerry G. *General Education Today.* San Francisco: Jossey-Bass Publishers, 1983.

Gans, Herbert J., Nathan Glazer, Joseph R. Gusfield, and Christopher Jencks, Eds. *On the Making of Americans: Essays in Honor of David Riesman.* University of Pennsylvania Press, Inc., 1979.

Gardner, John. *On Moral Fiction.* New York: Basic Books, 1978.

Goodlad, John I. *A Place Called School.* New York: McGraw-Hill, 1983.

Graham, Patricia Albjerg. "Schools: Cacophony about Practice, Silence about Purpose." *Daedalus,* Fall 1984.

Grant, Gerald. "The Teacher's Predicament." *Teacher's College Record,* Spring 1983.

———. "Children's Rights and Adult Confusions." *The Public Interest,* Fall 1982.

Hirsch, E. D., Jr. " 'English' and the Perils of Formalism." *The American Scholar,* Summer 1984.

Hook, Sidney. "Education in Defense of a Free Society." *Commentary,* July 1984.

Hosfar, Philip L., Ed. *Using What We Know About Teaching.* Alexandria, VA: Association for Supervision and Curriculum Development, 1984.

Howard, James, and Thomas Mendenhall. *Making History Come Alive: The Place of History in the Schools.* Washington, DC: Council for Basic Education, 1982.

Howard, John A., Ed. *On Freedom.* Greenwich, CT: Devin-Adair Publishers, 1984.

Hurd, Paul DeHart. "Reforming Science Education: The Search for a New Vision." Occasional Paper 33, Washington, DC: Council for Basic Education, 1984.

Kristol, Irving. *Reflections of a Neoconservative: Looking Back, Looking Ahead.* New York: Basic Books, 1983.

Kupperman, Joel J. *The Foundations of Morality.* London: George Allen & Unwin, 1983.

Ladner, Benjamin, Ed. *The Humanities in Precollegiate Education.* Chicago: National Society for the Study of Education, distributed by the University of Chicago Press, 1984.

Lightfoot, Sara Lawrence. *The Good High School: Portraits of Character and Culture.* New York: Basic Books, 1983.

MacIntyre, Alasdair. *After Virtue.* Notre Dame: Notre Dame Press, 1981.

Nisbet, Robert A. *The Sociological Tradition.* New York: Basic Books, 1966.

Oldenquist, Andrew. "The Decline of American Education in the 60s and 70s." *American Education,* May 1983.

Parr, Susan Resneck. *The Moral of the Story: Literature, Values, and American Education.* New York: Teachers College Press, 1982.

Partington, G. "Gramsci and Education." *Education Philosophy and Theory.* Summer 1981.

Peters, Thomas J., and Robert H. Waterman, Jr. *In Search of Excellence.* New York: Harper & Row, 1982.

Ravitch, Diane. *The Troubled Crusade: American Education, 1945–80.* New York: Basic Books, 1983.

———. *The Schools We Deserve: Reflections on the Educational Crises of Our Time.* New York: Basic Books, 1985.

Report of the National Commission on Excellence in Education. *A Nation at Risk: The Imperative for Educational Reform.* Washington, DC: U.S. Department of Education, 1983.

Report of the Twentieth Century Fund Task Force on Elementary and Secondary Education Policy. *Making the Grade.* New York: Twentieth Century Fund, 1983.

Rodriguez, Richard. *Hunger of Memory.* Boston: David R. Godine, 1982; New York: Bantam Books, 1982.

Rohlen, Thomas P. *Japan's High Schools.* Berkeley: University of California Press, 1983.

Sergiovanni, Thomas, J. "Leadership and Excellence in Schooling." *Educational Leadership,* February 1984.

Sewall, Gilbert T. *Necessary Lessons: Decline and Renewal in American Schools.* New York: The Free Press, 1983.

Sizer, Theodore R. *Horace's Compromise: The Dilemma of the American High School.* Boston: Houghton Mifflin, 1984.

Sommers, Christina Hoff. "Ethics Without Virtue: Moral Education in America." *The American Scholar,* Summer 1984.

Sowell, Thomas. "Black Excellence: The Case of Dunbar High School." *The Public Interest,* Spring 1974.

Sullivan, William M. *Reconstructing Public Philosophy.* Berkeley: University of California Press, 1982.

Zimiles, Herbert. "The Changing American Child: The Perspective of Educators." A report to the National Commission on Excellence in Education. October 1982.

✳

College admissions standards,
    86–87
College Board, 211
College English, 77
Colvin, Richard, 188
Commager, Henry Steele, 26
Communist Party, 63
Comparative Higher Education Research Group, 183
Comparison grouping, 123–124
Compulsory Mis-Education (Goodman), 11
Computers, 141, 173–175, 216
Computer science, 43, 62
Conformity, social, 36–37
Confucius, 39
Constitution, 48
    First Amendment, 93–94
Constitutional Rights Foundation,
    13
Cortines, Ray, 83, 145
Crane, Stephen: *The Red Badge of Courage,* 103
Crisis in the Classroom (Silberman),
    11
Cuban, Larry, 124–125
Cultural imperialism, 76–78
"Cultural literacy," 57
Culture against Man (Henry), 11
Curriculum, school
    federal aid for development,
        192–193
    monitoring, 170–171
    in "open education," 11–12
    reform, 43–45
    See also Traditional education

Daedalus, 77
Dance, 53
Darkness at Noon (Koestler), 103
Darwin, Charles, 201
Davis, Benjamin O., 72

"Deal, The," 84
"Death of a High School, The,"
    145
Declaration of Independence, 24,
    25, 48, 94
Democracy
    education and, 24–26, 33, 34,
        37–38, 63
    study of, 48
Departments of education, state,
    146–147
Deschooling movement, 205
Desegregation, 70
Deukmejian, George, 111, 115, 118
Diary of Anne Frank, The, 103
Dickens, Charles: *Bleak House,* 102
    Oliver Twist, 45
Dietz, Jim, 176
Disadvantaged students, 193–194
Discipline, school, 5, 130, 135–138,
    142, 171–172
Double Helix, The (Watson), 52
Douglass, Frederick, 65
Drew, Charles, 72
Drop-out rate, 74, 75
Drugs, 9, 106
"Dumbing down," 130, 133–134
Dunbar, Paul Laurence, 72
Dunbar High School, Washington,
    D.C., 71–73
Dundon, Ed., 145
Durkheim, Émile, 99
Dwight, Timothy, 198

Economics, 49
Educational Testing Service, 86
Education movements, 205–206
Education reporters, 188–189
Edward R. Murrow High School,
    Brooklyn, 73
Education Commission of the
    States, 3

Education and Ecstasy (Leonard), 11
Edwards, Harry, 86–87
El Camino High School, Sacramento, 109
Ellick, Tom, 176
English
  as core subject, 43, 45–47
  and moral code, 102–103
Ethics, 39–40, 91–94, 100–107
  See also Morality
Excellence movement, 71–76, 85, 161
  See also Traditional education

Fallon, Mike, 133–134
Family breakup, 9
Fathers and Sons (Turgenev), 45
Federal government
  and educational reform, 189–195
  funding for curriculum development, 192–193
Federalist Papers, 48
Field Poll, 5, 110, 125
Fine arts, 53
Finn, Chester E., Jr., 81
First Interstate, 165
"Five New Basics," 43
Florida
  Association of Black Psychologists, 85
  career ladders in, 157
  reform in, 204
  testing in, 85
Fluor, Bob, 117, 118
Fluor Corporation, 117, 118
Foreign languages, 52–53
Fortune, 199
Frady, Marshall, 189
Frankfurter, Justice Felix, 136
Free school movement, 205

Funding for public schools, 110–111, 146, 175–176
  cuts, 110, 191
  by federal government, 190

Gallup Polls
  on education, 22, 94–95, 164
  on voucher plan, 70
General Motors, 28
Geography, 48
Getty, Ann, 176
Gifford, Bernard, 86
Golden State Exams, 141
Goodman, Paul: *Compulsory Mis-Education,* 11
Grading, 42–43
Graduation requirements, 4, 10, 160, 170
Graham, Patricia Albjerg, 77
Gramsci, Antonio, 79
Great Britain, 23, 201–202

Haldane, J. B. S.: "On Being the Right Size," 46
Haley, Alex: *Roots,* 81
Handler, Harry, 145
Harris Poll, 160–161
Hart, Gary (state senator), 114, 151
Harvey, James, 118
Hastee, William H., 72
Heald Colleges, 176
Health classes, 53, 54
Henderson, Laverta, 169
Henry, Jules: *Culture against Man,* 11
Henry V (Shakespeare), 103
Herndon, Terry, 140
Hewlett-Packard, 118, 205
High-technology industries, 212–213
Hirsch, E. D., Jr., 57
Hispanic students, 71, 76, 83, 113

History/Social Science
  as core course, 47–49, 63
  "no-fault history," 103–104
  stereotypes in, 81
  ethics through, 65
  teaching with video, 175
Holbo, Paul S., 185
Holocaust, 103–104
Holt, John: *How Children Fail,* 11,
  13, 79
Homework, 5, 130, 138–139, 142,
  172
  in Japanese schools, 29
Honig, Nancy, 115–116, 176
How Children Fail (Holt), 11, 79
Huckleberry Finn (Twain), 45
Hughes, Teresa, 114
Humanities, 42, 189–190
  ethics through, 100–107
  in traditional education, 63–67
Hunt, Robert M., 103
Hunter's Point, 14, 102
Huntington Beach School District,
  110

IBM, 205
Illiteracy, 71
Immigrants, 31–32
Individualism, 91–93, 101–102
Industrial Revolution, 48
Innovation in traditional education,
  16–18
In Search of Excellence (Peters and
  Waterman), 147, 186
International Education Achieve-
  ment study, 31
Irving, Washington: *The Legend of
  Sleepy Hollow,* 46

Jackson, Jesse, 77
Japan, 27, 28, 29–31, 158, 178
Japan's High Schools (Rohlen), 30

Jefferson, Thomas, 25–26, 38, 203
Job growth, projected, 212–215
Job obsolescence, 61
Job openings projected for
  1982–1995 (Table), 215
Jobs in United States, 1982 (Table),
  214
John Swett Elementary School, 13
Jones, James Earl, 77
Jonson, Ben, 202
Juvenal, 53

Kaiser Aluminum, 118
Kant, Immanuel, 65
Kentucky, reform in, 204
Kern County Alliance for Quality
  Schools, 117
King, Martin Luther, Jr., 48, 80
Knapp, Randy, 176
Kobe University entrance exam, 30
Koestler, Arthur: *Darkness at Noon,*
  103
Kohlberg, Lawrence, 98
Korea, students in, 178

Language mastery, 7–8, 58–60, 64
Laws mandating public education,
  24
Law of the Twelve Tablets, 26
Legend of Sleepy Hollow, The (Irv-
  ing), 46
LeNoir, Michael, 69–70
Leonard, George: *Education and Ec-
  stasy,* 11
Levin, Henry, 37, 211–216
Lincoln, Abraham, 80
Lindbergh, Charles, 104
Lippmann, Walter, 101
Literacy, 56
  "cultural literacy," 57

Literature
  as teacher of ethics, 65–67,
    102–103
  See also English
Little Women (Alcott), 46
Locke, John, 24
Lockheed, 118, 205
Loevenger, Jane, 98
Looking Out For Number One, 38
Los Angeles Education Partnership,
  205
Los Angeles times, 118, 188
Lowell High School, San Francisco,
  15
Lucas, George, 175
Lutheran vernacular schools, 24

McGuffey's Reader, 100
Macy's, 118
Magnet school movement, 201
Magowan, Peter, 118
Maier, Cornell, 118
Mann, Horace, 26, 36
Marin County, 17, 124
Markham Elementary School, Oak-
  land, 169
Marx, Karl, 215
  theory of education, 79–80
Massachusetts Board of Education,
  26
Massachusetts General School Act
  of 1647, 24
Mathematics, 42
  as core subject, 43, 49–51
  federal aid for teachers, 191
  teacher shortage, 153
Matthiessen, Peter: *Sal Si Puedes,* 81
Mechanical drawing, 62
Media and educational reform,
  187–189
Medusa and the Snail, The (Thomas),
  46

Mengele, Josef, 64
Menlo Park Elementary School, 110
"Mentor teachers," 119–120, 149,
  157–158
Merit pay, 22, 158, 160
Mesa, Pete, 83
Milipitas School District, 83, 106
Minimum competency movement,
  85, 205
Minority students
  in California, 113
  public education and, 69–73
  and SAT scores, 9, 71
  traditional education for, 74–89
Modesto City Unified School Dis-
  trict, 110
Montesquieu, Charles Louis de Se-
  condat, 24
Morality
  instilled in public education, 8,
    36, 38–40, 91–107, 201
  pattern of development in chil-
    dren, 98
  traditional education and, 64–67
Moral Majority, 92
Music, 53

"Nation at Risk, A," 187
  See President's Commission on
    Excellence in Education
National Academy of Science, 211
National Assessment of Educational
  Performance, 55–56
National Center for Education Sta-
  tistics, 43, 51, 75
National Center for Neighborhood
  Enterprise, 70
National Commission on Secondary
  Schooling for Hispanics,
  204–205
National Education Association,
  140, 160

National Endowment for the Humanities, 189
National Science Foundation, 3, 192
Native Americans, 76
Native Son (Wright), 81
Natural sciences, 42
Nazis, 34
New Jersey v. *T.L.O.*, 138
New Orleans, 70
Newsweek, 3
1984 (Orwell), 64
Nisei Daughter (Sone), 81
"No-fault history," 103–104
Norris, Frank: *The Octopus*, 103

Oakland, California, 194
  Oakland School District, 167
Oakland Tribune, 169, 188
Octopus, The (Norris), 103
Oliver Twist (Dickens), 45
"On Being the Right Size" (Haldane), 46
"Open education," 11–12, 14–15, 205
Orwell, George: *Animal Farm*, 45
  1984, 64
Overfelt High School, San Jose, 143–144
Ox Bow Incident, The (Clark), 102

Pacho (Villareal), 81
Parents
  importance of, 163–167, 177–179
  increasing involvement of, 168–173, 175–177
Parochial schools, 154
"Path Study," 43–45, 110
Payzant, Tom, 145
Peters, Thomas: *In Search of Excellence*, 147, 186, 187
Physical education, 53–54
Physics, 51

Piaget, Jean, 97–98
Pioneer High School, 119, 190
Politics
  in classroom, 104–105
  and support of schools, 175–177
Prayer in schools, 105
President's Commission on Excellence in Education, 3, 4, 43, 56, 119, 177, 187
Price, Leontyne, 177
Principals, school, 143–145, 172, 191–192
Private schools, 54–55
  tax credits for, 191
Pro-education rallies, 176–177
Progressive, 79
Promotion policies, 50
Proposition 13, 110, 146
Public education, United States, 24–26
  instills morality, 8, 36, 38–40, 91–107, 201
  and minority students, 69–73
  purpose of, 23, 26–40
  and social mobility, 203–204
Public Interest, The (periodical), 71

Quality Education Project (QEP), 167–169, 176–177
Quintilian, 7–8

Racism, 75–88
Ratio Studiorum (St. Ignatius of Loyola), 26
Ravitch, Diana, 183, 205–206
  The Troubled Crusade: American Education 1945–80, 10
"Readability formula," 13
Reading, 56–57
  reading programs, 45–46

Reagan, Ronald, 3, 118–119, 190, 203
  budget for fiscal 1986, 191
Red Badge of Courage, The (Crane, 103
Reed Union School District, 17–18, 124
Reform, education
  in California, 4, 109–126, 205
  curriculum reform, 43–45
  implementing, 141–147
  media and, 187–189
  opposition to, 21–22, 151, 158–161, 185–187
  tools of, 130–142
Reichardt, Carl, 118
Reilly, Clint, 5
Religion
  and public education, 24
  in schools, 93–94, 105
Remarque, Erich: *All Quiet on the Western Front,* 103
Report cards, 11
Robertson, Jeanne, 176
Robert Taylor Hones housing project, 73
Rohlen, Thomas: *Japan's High Schools,* 30
Roman Empire, 48
Roots (Haley), 81
"Rule by law" school discipline, 136
"Rule by personality" school discipline, 136
Rumberger, Russell, 37, 211–216
Russell, Bertrand, 49

Sacramento Press Club, 111
Sacramento Union, 133
Safeway, 118, 165
St. Ignatius of Loyola: *Ratio Studiorum,* 26

Salaries, teachers', 153, 155
Sal Si Puedes (Matthiessen), 81
Salter, Kit, 185
Samurai of Gold Hill (Ushida), 81
San Francisco Examiner, 137
San Jose Mercury News, 124
San Jose School District, 83, 110
San Juan School District, 158
SAT. *See* Scholastic Aptitude Test
Savage, David, 188
Schlein, Phil, 118
Scholastic Aptitude Test (SAT)
  California scores, 121
  drop in scores, 4, 8–9, 55
  1982 scores, 71
  prospective teachers' scores, 152
  and textbooks used, 58
School boards, 144, 145
School Boards Association, 112
School districts, 144–145
  funding by, 110, 146
School principals, 143–145, 172, 191–192
Schools of education, 156, 183, 185–187
Science
  as core subject, 43, 51–52
  federal aid for teachers, 191
  and NSF programs, 192
Second Community School, 14, 16, 200
Shakespeare, William: *Henry V,* 103
Shanker, Albert, 149, 161
Sheinbaum, Stanley, 117
Silberman, Charles: *Crisis in the Classroom,* 11, 13
Silicon Valley, 114, 205
Simon, Sidney, 95
Slavery, 65
Social conformity, 36–37
Social equality through education, 13, 80, 88, 203–204

✳

Social identities, 27–28, 31–32,
  34–35
Social mobility, 203–204
Social Science/History, 43, 47–49
  See also History/Social Science
Sone, Monica: *Nisei Daughter,* 81
Sowell, Thomas, 71–73
Special interest groups, 131–132,
  175–176
Special needs students, 176
  programs for, 191, 193
Stages of Reading Development
  (Chall), 56
Standard Brands Paint, 118
Stanford University
  Institute for Research on Educa-
    tion, Finance, and Governance,
    37, 211–215
  "Path Study," 43–45, 110
  School of Education, 124, 155
States
  departments of education,
    146–147
  funding for education, 110,
    175–176, 190
Stemple, John, 145
Stevenson, Robert Louis: *Treasure
  Island,* 46
Stewart, Fred, 145
Story of Our Country, The, 16
Students
  changes in, 177–178
  disadvantaged, 193–194
  special needs, 176, 191, 193
"Subject matter competency," 156
Suicide, 106
Sykes, Gary, 84

Teacher competency exams
  in California, 86, 88, 151
  in Florida, 85
Teacher Corps, Cycle 5, 13

Teachers, 147
  education and training, 156–157,
    182–185
  and "failed revolutions," 205–206
  oppose reform, 149–151
  qualities of good teacher, 151–153
  recruiting, 155
  salaries, 153, 155
  sources of dissatisfaction, 154
  unions, 22, 158–161
Teaching machine movement, 161,
  205
Teilheit, Raoul, 161
Television viewing, 9, 165–167
Tennessee, career ladders in, 157
Tenure, 112, 159
Testing, 130, 140–141, 160
Texas, education reform in, 204
Textbooks, 130–135, 142, 171
  "dumbing down," 130, 133–134
  scarcity of, 110
Theatre, 53
Thinking, independent, 7, 63–64
  importance of, 58–59
Thomas, Lewis: *The Medusa and the
  Snail,* 46
Time, 3
Time-allocation chart, 171
"Tough-love" policies, 83
Tracking school progress, 121, 122
"Tracks" of school population,
  43–44, 202
Traditional education
  for character formation, 64–67,
    99
  core subjects, 45–54, 129
  for good citizenship, 62–64
  innovations in, 16–18
  for minorities, 74–89
  why it works, 55–60
  for workers, 60–62
Transamerica, 118

Traumatola, Larry, 167–168
Treasure Island (Stevenson), 46
Trinidad, Reuben, 143
Troubled Crusade: The, American Education 1945–80 (Ravitch), 10
TRW, 205
Tubman, Harriet, 65
Tucker, Gene, 145
Turgenev, Ivan: *Fathers and Sons,* 45
Twain, Mark: *Huckleberry Finn,* 45
Twentieth Century Fund, 3
Typing, 62

Unions, teachers', 22, 151, 158–161
Union of Soviet Socialist Republics (U.S.S.R.), 48, 63
United States Chamber of Commerce, 62
United States (government)
  Bureau of Labor Statistics, 28
  projections, 37, 212
  Department of Education, 175, 189, 194, 204
  Supreme Court
  New Jersey v. *T.L.O.,* 138
  1969 decision on school discipline, 135–136
United States history, study of, 48, 63
Universities
  functions of, 181–182
  and teacher training, 183–187
University of California system, 182
  Berkeley, 153–154
University of Massachusetts School of Education, 95
Ushida, Yoshiko: *Samurai of Gold Hill,* 81

"Values clarification," 17, 95–99
Vietnam War, 9–10, 32
Villareal, Jose: *Pacho,* 81
Visual arts, 53
Vocational education, 61–62
Voucher system, 199–200

Walberg, Herbert, 139, 163–164
Wallenberg, Raoul, 104
Wall Street Journal, 202
Watergate, 9
Waterman, Robert: *In Search of Excellence,* 147, 186, 187
Watrous, Mary Woodworth, 202–203
Watson, James: *The Double Helix,* 52
Weaver, Robert C., 72
Wells Fargo Bank, 118
Wespercorp, 176
Western Addition of San Francisco, 13
Willie, Charles, 82
Winthrop, John, 48
Wirtz, Willard, 9
Women in teaching, 153
Workers, 27–29, 37
  traditional education for, 60–62
World history, 48–49
World War II, 34
Wright, Richard: *Native Son,* 81
Writing, 46–47, 58–59

Young, John, 118
Young, Michael, F. D., 79

Zimales, Herbert, 177–178